Praise for *Reset Your Legacy*

Dr Gerdi van den Berg's book, *Reset Your Legacy*, offers a profound guide for those seeking to navigate life's complexities through the power of prayer.

This book invites readers to step into the sacred role of an intercessor – one who stands in the gap, praying fervently for themselves and their loved ones to fulfil the unique destiny God has designed for them. It is not merely a manual for prayer; it is a roadmap for spiritual growth, healing, and transformation.

Dr van den Berg merges her profound understanding of human psychology and her unwavering commitment to the truth of God's Word. Each phase, from preconception to the final steps of earthly life, is explored with care, revealing the spiritual, emotional, and physical dynamics at play.

The beauty of this journey lies in its holistic approach, where prayer becomes a tool to not only shape future generations but also to restore and redeem the past. She wisely reminds us, while we cannot change the past, we can alter its impact on our lives and the lives of those we hold dear through prayer and the help of the Holy Spirit. While reading through the phases, she equips readers with the tools to pray intentionally, apply key Scriptures and reflect on personal insights.

At the heart of this book is an invitation to meet with God, to align our personal stories with His grand narrative, to hear His voice, and to enter into a deeper, more intimate fellowship with Him. Each chapter resonates with this call to restore brokenness, nurture growth and reclaim the destiny God has spoken over each life.

It is with great honour that I present *Reset Your Legacy* to you. May this book inspire you to pray with new depth, to love more fully and to find healing as you discover God's heart for your life and the lives of those you cherish.

Dr Gerdi van den Berg is a dear friend, a mentor and someone I look up to and learn from. Thank you so much for being obedient to the voice of the Holy Spirit and writing this book. I am grateful to have you in my life!

> *– Marietjie Malan, congregation leader with her husband, Marius Malan, at Kompas Gemeente, Vanderbijlpark, South Africa*

This book invites readers to embark on a profound journey through the twelve phases of human development, from pre-conception to legacy. Each phase is meticulously explored, revealing the intricate interplay between spiritual, emotional, and physical growth. With sensitivity and expertise, Dr van den Berg provides tools for focused prayer, empowering readers to unlock the full potential of their loved ones and themselves.

Reset Your Legacy is more than a book — it is an invitation to join the greatest story ever told. It is a call to reclaim the narrative of our lives, to reframe our experiences and to rediscover our true identity in Christ. As we pray through these twelve phases, we will find ourselves drawn closer to the Father's heart, hearing His voice, and living with fearless, whole and healed hearts.

Our understanding, gained through working in more than 100 countries with *The World Needs a Father* is that every human being lives with insecurities caused by father and mother wounds.

Dr van den Berg's book certainly is a must-read and will go a long way to help heal and empower those living with insecurities, and if you embark on this journey early enough it will lay a good foundation for the next generation to thrive.

– Vian and Riette Storm, Global coordinators of The World needs a Father

Strategic prayer to navigate
through 12 phases of development

Reset Your
LEGACY

DR GERDI VAN DEN BERG

GLOBAL
PUBLISHING

RESET YOUR LEGACY
Strategic prayer to navigate through 12 phases of development

Text © Gerdi van den Berg 2024

Published by Global Publishing, an imprint of Global Publishing Partners, LLC Nashville, TN, USA

First edition 2024

Designed by Bateleur Media and Publishing (Pty.) Ltd., Cape Town, South Africa.

Bible quotations marked AMPC are from *Amplified Bible, Classic Edition* copyright © 1954, 1958, 1962, 1964, 1965, 1987 by The Lockman Foundation. Used with permission. All rights reserved.
Bible quotations marked MSG are from *The Message*, copyright © 1993, 2002, 2018 by Eugene H. Peterson.
Used with permission. All rights reserved.
Bible quotations marked AMP are from *Amplified Bible*, copyright © 2015 by The Lockman Foundation,
La Habra, CA 90631. Used with permission. All rights reserved.
Bible quotations marked KJV are from *King James Version*, Public Domain.
Bible quotations marked TPT are from *The Passion Translation*® is a registered trademark of Passion & Fire Ministries, Inc.
Copyright © 2020 Passion & Fire Ministries, Inc. Used with permission. All rights reserved.
Bible quotations marked Mirror Bible are from *Mirror Study Bible*, © Mirror Word 2022 by Francois du Toit.
Used with permission. All rights reserved.

All emphasis within Bible quotations is the author's own.

Cover image designed by Magriki
Cover and inside design by Monique Bijker
Illustration on page 160 © Kompas Gemeente
Author image by Brenda Veldtman Photography

ISBN: 979-8-89317-102-0

I dedicate this book to my parents, Chris and Jossie Theron,
who during their earthly stay faithfully covered our present and future generations
in dedicated prayer. May their legacy bring glory to our King!

I entrust *Reset Your Legacy* to the One who loves hearing our voice,
and who continues to encourage and inspire us to bring our heart cries before Him;
the One who beautifies our stories: the one and only living Creator God.

I have no greater joy than this; to hear that my [spiritual] children are living their lives in the Truth.

— 3 JOHN 1:4, AMPC

Acknowledgements

With any journey, there are easy walks, steep hills and tough climbs. It is, however, the company that makes the journey rich and fulfilling, especially when scaling the cliffs or descending into the valleys. I therefore want to thank all my co-travellers: the mothers and fathers who carry the weight of responsible love, the prayer warriors who never cease and who dare to trust that He loves our children more than we will ever be able to.

Thank you to my husband, Cobus, whose passion to see the following generations flourish makes him an encouraging co-traveller. It is an absolute privilege to journey through life together.

Thank you to my children, Christiaan, Lorraine, Llewellyn, Johan and Daniela, and my grandson, Milas. You enrich my life with joy and celebration. I am forever grateful for the calling to prayerfully watch over you. May you continue to live life passionately and enjoy the fruit of generational prayers. May you also continue to keep these prayer altars burning for the generations to come!

A deep, heartfelt "thank you" to all my prayer partners' continuous encouragement and for eagerly warring with me! We are forever connected.

Thank you to my editor and publisher, Antoinette le Roux, for being a co-journer in far more than the publishing of this book. I have huge admiration and appreciation for your dedication, work ethic and wisdom!

Dearest reader, to you my sincerest gratitude! May all the prayer seeds you sow bring a rich harvest of God-honouring souls, now and for generations to come. Let your prayer voice be heard!

Contents

Introduction to This Journey

Who controls the past, controls the future.
Who controls the present, controls the past.
– GEORGE ORWELL

The Call

Today, more than ever, there is a need for faithful prayer warriors to move into their godly position as intercessors, to pray for the restoration and redemption of the next generation, and to be drawn closer to our Father's heart as they hear His voice. A call to lovingly obey Him and to enjoy fellowship with Jesus with a fearless, whole heart.

This is a call to be a warrior (not a worrier) in the Kingdom. If you view life and this journey in the light of who He is, the joy of being part of His recreative ability will energise you to keep pursuing His truth, no matter the cost. He is a timeless Creator and Re-Creator, rewriting the future of your history.

The Why, How and What of Your Prayer Journey

WHY YOU ARE GOING ON THIS JOURNEY

It was one of those rare windless, mid-summer days, and the sea had the appearance of a lake with none of the typical loud splashing of waves. I could easily focus on writing this and what I was pondering in my heart. My thoughts were full of multiple conversations I'd had the privilege of being part of in all my years of being a therapist. They often overlapped in content, not because people carry similar stories, but because the imprint of pain is so similar.

When broken-hearted parents are on my couch, there is an alignment between my heart and theirs. I feel their pain, their fear, and their hopelessness and desperation. What if they are not as helpless as they feel? What if they can take the position as co-workers in the Kingdom and grasp the power of prayer? What if . . .?

Our Saviour came to save, to redeem and to renew. In *Reset Your Legacy*, I discuss how this reality can manifest in the lives of those we care passionately about.

I have divided man's journey on earth into twelve different phases, which may or may not align with current psychological viewpoints. Although a vast amount of research forms part of the content, it is not the intention to present a psychological or biological manual on developmental stages. Please consider these twelve phases as merely providing guidelines for focused prayer.

In each stage of development, the specific aspects involved on a spiritual, emotional and physical level are mentioned, as well as how this information can be applied in effective prayer. Tools for focused prayer will therefore be provided and discussed as you journey through these phases. You can either use these tools in preparation for marriage and/or having children, or you can, like most of us on this journey, use the tools to restore the damage of the past. The past cannot be changed, BUT the impact of the past can.

Therefore, dear fellow traveller, *what is the potential of your own and your child's history? Where will the interpretation of his past lead him?*

This course aims to realign you and your loved one's history to His Story of redemption.

Intercession shakes history!
~ CINDY JACOBS

During this journey, you return to the beginning of your loved one's timeline (only for a while) and start praying over certain aspects that occurred then. Returning to the beginning does not mean that you view the past as more significant than the present or the future. A return entails identifying relevant experiences that may be harmful and limiting at the present time. This may include anything that warps the truth. Addressing these specifically in the light of God's truth is the purpose of this journey.

Remember: History consists of events and their impact, and the impact depends on our interpretation. It is the interpretation that packages these experiences in our hearts. Our hearts contain our story and our convictions.

Experiences of abuse in its various forms will damage or greatly challenge the truth. However, it is not the experience that causes long-term damage; it is rather the interpretation of the experience that does the damage by distorting our self-definition, our perceptions of God, of life in general and of who others are. Our views then move out of their original alignment with the truth, and past pain becomes the dictator of the future. Realignment is thus required to restore these distortions.

We cannot change the past, but we *can* change its impact.

So, let's revisit our history for a bit – only so that we can align it with the Father's truth regarding *Who He is* and *Who we are in Him*.

In each of the twelve phases, there are processes that are aimed at unlocking our full potential – not merely surviving life's challenges, but unlocking and enjoying the fulfilment and blessings our Creator intended for us.

It is rewriting the future of our history and that of our loved ones.

David declared in Psalm 18:24, MSG, "God rewrote the text of my life when I opened the book of my heart to his eyes."

Reconsolidation, a term used in psychology, sheds beautiful light on what happens during change or rewriting, as we read in this Psalm. *Consolidation* is the term for the long-term capturing of memories. Reconsolidation occurs when we revisit the happenings of the past, as stored in our memory banks, and rewrite the interpretation of those experiences in a new and hopefully redeemed version (see Romans 12:2).

As an interceding parent, we move into this position and activate Father God's recreative power in our loved ones' lives. Mothers are appointed as the main intercessors for their family, whether they realise this or not. A mother carries the highest ranking as intercessor; she is the watchman for the family. She nurtures, comforts and serves the physical, emotional and spiritual needs of her beloved family.

> We cannot change the past, but we *can* change its impact.

God's precious Holy Spirit is also *your* Intercessor. He is the one brooding (hovering) over barrenness, bringing forth life (see Genesis 1:2).

The word for "hovering" in Hebrew is *rachaph*, indicating fluttering or moving to and fro with the purpose of creating waves of energy. This type of energy creates, and it brings forth life and change!

Fathers are the protectors and the blessers. Their opinions, words and presence play a vital role in the child's gradual moving into adulthood and the imprint of identity made on their heart's tablets. Fathers "write" with words and with non-verbal communication through their behaviour. They also "write" with regular intentional prayer, proclamations and affirmations for and over their children.

To enter and operate from these positions can activate and result in the rewriting of your loved one's story, including reconsolidating the impact of the experiences that happened, or that should have happened but did not.

The same story, but a redeemed version!

This is WHY we are going on this journey.

THE WHAT OF THIS JOURNEY

A phase is a slice of time that consists of certain trademarks and aspects of life that should typically occur during that period of development. These will include unavoidable external aspects. Each phase presents life-based or community requirements, challenging the individual to meet certain physical, spiritual, mental and emotional goals. This book aims to unpack the individual and environmental expectations during each phase of development, and will provide and support parents/loved ones/intercessors with the required prayer points. The impact of meeting specific needs during each phase, as well as neglect-impact (for whatever reason), will form part of the prayer points.

During each phase, the physical, emotional, mental and spiritual aspects of development will be addressed, as well as various environmental factors that apply and/or are required for functional development during that phase.

The process entails the arrival at the new phase and being ready and prepared to unlock what that phase holds. The person's potential should be unlocked by the various role-players who are active in that phase, in order to reveal and activate the treasures within. The unlocking enables the inflow of the necessary "equipment" required to develop effectively during that phase.

Vast amounts of research data are included in the abovementioned; however, as is the case with all research data, it is based on the current research hypothesis, analysis and conclusions available at the time of writing. Remember that research is ongoing and will always require updating. Some research links have been provided as endnotes at the end of each chapter and others are mentioned in between the writings. More research articles can be found on my website, *Heart Matters*, for which a QR code has been provided at the back of this book.

I enthusiastically encourage you, the reader, to dive into your own research adventures if the interest is there, and to share with me as you please. We are all discovering and learning together.

How a child develops into adulthood largely depends on the role-players, who have huge responsibilities and who form part of the external factors that impact each phase. You will look at these closely along your journey.

You will see how important certain behavioural patterns are. There are distinct behaviours that have either a damaging or an empowering impact. Look at them closely in order to pray with understanding.

This journey will inevitably shine the light on mistakes we as parents have made, some knowingly, others very much without the required insight at the time. Please remember that this is not a journey of recrimination, riddled with guilt for mistakes and "I-shouldn't-haves". But it *is* a journey of working through these mistakes hand in hand with the Father's gentle and merciful Holy Spirit, enjoying the impact of redemption for yourself and for the ones you are standing in the gap for. Such change carries eternal value.

Although we will peer into the past regarding the relevant impact points, this prayer journey should stay strictly on track towards a realigned future.

This is mostly a walking-back journey in order to freely move forward.

THE JOURNEY

You are on this journey with one primary goal in mind: to face Him – the Author and Finisher of you and your loved ones' destinies.

Every journey has a starting point and is completed by taking one step at a time. The more you value the journey itself, the more you will embrace the details shared along the way. Appreciation opens the heart for revelation. Invite His light to reveal your mistakes, remembering that you need never feel ashamed.

> *For the Word that God speaks is alive and full of power [making it active, operative, energizing, and effective]; it is sharper than any two-edged sword, penetrating to the dividing line of the breath of life (soul) and [the immortal] spirit, and of joints and marrow [of the deepest parts of our nature], exposing and sifting and analyzing and judging the very thoughts and purposes of the heart.*
>
> *And not a creature exists that is concealed from His sight, but all things are open and exposed, naked and defenseless to the eyes of Him with Whom we have to do.*
>
> *For we do not have a High Priest Who is unable to understand and sympathize and have a shared feeling with our weaknesses and infirmities and liability to the assaults of temptation, but One Who has been tempted in every respect as we are, yet without sinning.*
>
> — HEBREWS 4:12, 13, 15, AMPC

We serve a Father who encourages honesty and truth. Being the kindest of gentlemen, He eagerly waits for your permission to open the pathway to your heart. He desires this for the sole purpose of healing and bringing you into deeper alignment with His truth in order to know Him.

You may feel overwhelmed, not knowing where to begin to pray for your children and loved ones. This book can be the starting point.

As you journey, continuously ask Father God to shine His light on those areas that need to be addressed – no matter what they may contain.

This is a journey where you will often need to stand still, be still, quieten your inner thoughts, and listen. Allow the Holy Spirit to hover over the phase you are working through and gently drop His revelations into your heart, sometimes via a conversation with a relative, by looking at a photo, or just by picking up on things in casual chats. Your eyes and ears will be attuned to this information. They are the keys to unlock.

Throughout this journey, you need to mentally calibrate to see whether the piece of information you are working with is in line with His truth. Is this what it should be in the light of the Word and the redemptive work of Jesus? If not, realignment is required and recreation will take place.

As the intercessor, you confess the exposed sin on behalf of your loved ones, yourself and, where appropriate, your predecessors. Repent and gratefully accept His gift of forgiveness.

As you journey, keep the following in mind:

- You become aware of your own mistakes and/or the sin committed against you and also against your loved ones – knowingly or not.
- If you commit these to God, you own up, acknowledge and confront them. Be real and honest.
- You bring them before Him, your Saviour and Redeemer.
- You ask forgiveness.
- Gratefully accept His forgiveness and forgive yourself and all others involved.
- You move on – free from the guilt, judgement and shame!

KEY SCRIPTURES	
1 John 1:9	Psalm 3:3

You may then invite the recreative power of the Holy Spirit to restore. Take authority over the relevant situation and bring it into subjection to what His Truth is. This is when reconsolidation occurs.

The rewriting of your child's (his)story occurs as it continues to align with His Story, bit by bit, phase by phase.

It is the same story, but a redeemed version!

The Twelve Phases

THE THREE PARTS:

Part 1: Arrive	Part 2: Receive	Part 3: Influence
Phase 1: Pre-conception	Phase 5: First 3 years	Phase 9: 13–18 years
Phase 2: Conception	Phase 6: 3–6 years	Phase 10: 18–35 years
Phase 3: In the Womb	Phase 7: 6–12 years	Phase 11: 35–55 years
Phase 4: Birth	Phase 8:12–13 years	Phase 12: 55+ years

- Please note that the male gender has been applied to any mention of the loved one for which you will be interceding. This is purely for less cluttered reading and does not carry any gender bias, or a disregard for both genders, as God created both male and female.
- The symbols used in the discussions of each phase include:

 The content of the phase.

 That which can be used to unlock the required potential of your loved one during a particular phase. It will therefore highlight the various prayer points.

◁▭ Personal notes you discover or remember as you journey through that phase.

- **Prayers:** It is best to use your own words and heart cries. Apply the Word of God to the appropriate key points. Use the prayers merely as guidelines.
- **Notes:** Delve into this journey and make it yours in every sense, keeping prayer notes.

A Prayer Before You Embark on This Journey

MY All-powerful Creator God, You are the Covenant-keeping God and I serve you with an eager heart. Thank you for the complete redemptive work of Your Son, my Saviour Jesus Christ!

Thank you, my Father, that You are not bound by time. You are, in fact, the Creator of time and space, including all concepts of past, present and future.

Because You are the Beginning and the End, the Alpha and Omega, You are in absolute control of time. Therefore, my King, I trust You to move back on the timelines I am bringing before You – to restore any damage done. May every dot on this line be redeemed to bring You glory!

I welcome Your light and truth (see Hebrews 4:12–15).

I give You permission to enter my own and our past with Your restorative power, to align and renew each one's history to Your redemptive story!

May our past rest in Who You are!

I choose to fix my eyes on You, the beginning and the end, our Re-Creator, Re-Aligner, Forerunner and timeless God!

I mention my loved one's name(s) before You now, LORD:

I ask for Your protection for all involved. I also ask for protection against clutter and feelings of being overwhelmed, burdened, judged and despondent. Help me, Lord, not to focus on sin and our sinfulness and so be deceived, but to bring it before you swiftly in order to receive forgiveness and to keep moving forward.

Please guide me, Father God, not to stand still where I should move on and not to move on when I have to pause. Constantly bring Your recreative power into this process and guide me clearly according to my capacity and Your love for me.

I also ask for Your anointing, Father – for courage, discipline, steadfastness, hope, faith, trust and patience.

Open my heart's eyes and ears to see and hear what Your light and Word reveals.
I submit to Your Truth, Father God, and willingly embark on this prayer journey. Thank you for being more committed to me and my loved ones' wholeness than I can ever be.
In Jesus' powerful Name I pray. Amen.

KEY SCRIPTURES	
Ephesians 3:20	1 John 5:14

PART 1

Arrive

Life is about moments;
never underestimate your moments in prayer.

The *Arrive* part consists of the first four phases: pre-conception, conception, womb period and birth. It is the preparation part of your journey. Birth is the triumph of arrival. Your loved one announces, "I am here. Finally! Hello, world!" It should be entered into with an eager sense of expectation.

To reach a place requires a destination. The desired or feared line has to be crossed over: desired because you are welcome and safe; feared because preparing for arrival is not aligned with destiny.

Impact is unavoidable whether you are welcome, unexpected or unwelcome. It leaves invisible footprints that others will follow. May this prayer journey cause such followers to reach the most profound destination where you will always be welcome, safe and truly loved. Home.

The *Arrive* part of the twelve-phase journey reveals the intent of the role-players in the history of the loved one. Looking forward (towards the future), this part demands strategic preparation for the new role of parenthood. Looking back (towards the past), the *Arrive* part may remind or uncover undesirable aspects of you or your loved one's history.

This is the opportunity to confront and pray through that which needs realignment. Be continuously reminded that history does not define you or your loved one. Only the One who Created humanity has the authority to define and redefine.

KEY SCRIPTURES	
Proverbs 8	Psalm 139

As you embark on this journey, investigating the impact of the phases of preparation, keep your heart focused on the One who designed and formed life. May His words over-rule the accusations and deceptions of the past and unlock the godly potential hidden in each one of us.

Phase 1: Pre-conception

PREPARATION

We serve the God of Abraham, Isaac and Jacob.

He is a God of generations. Promises made to one generation includes and impacts the next. Like a filling up and spilling over, the blessings overflow and often multiply from generation to generation.

There are godly principles applicable where generations are involved, purely because our Father is a deeply caring and loving Father. He desires His offspring to benefit from His seed.

Phase 1 is a foundational phase and a vital preparation for the next generation. You may need to pause at any relevant aspects from past generations.

It will be during this phase that the foundation of this journey is moulded and shaped into a new redeemed version. A strong foundation is non-negotiable when establishing a secure structure on which it is built. It is therefore wise to attend wholeheartedly to this first phase and seek Him for revelation. The Pre-conception Phase is often one of the most hidden phases of development.

Phase 1 is the preparation for the generations ahead, and "preparation" will be the main theme for this phase.

What Does Pre-conception Contain/Hold?

Pre is the adverb used when a chronological aspect is involved; something happens before something else. In this case, the very first phase to be discussed is the phase occurring before conception. It will pave the way for the following phases and, as you journey, it will probably show up every so often with relevant data.

The content of this phase exists purely of environmental factors, some of which lie outside human control, while others may be fully manageable by the relevant role-players. Both act as keys that unlock creational gold.

The primary human factors involved during this phase include generational lineages filled with stories of triumphs and devastations, faith-filled testimonies and deep disappointments in spiritual prayer expectations, normalities and absurdities.

Predictability often attempts to define normality: If you follow the same steps and get the same results, it is viewed as normal. This kind of normality creates some level of security. However, what is viewed as "normal" in God's eyes? Life, in general, is unpredictable and risky. Most of our circumstances lie outside our control. There are, however, a certain number of aspects in life we can control, such as thoughts, faith, convictions, behaviour, attitude and friendships. Still, none of them lie within your loved one's grasp during *this* phase or the next.

Other aspects also outside your loved ones' control are other's choices, circumstances prior to conception, family lineages and dynamics, as well as words spoken by relevant ones regarding the next generations. The general uncontrollables, although loaded with impact, would be environmental circumstances such as wars, natural disasters, economic environments and other factors affecting the chance of healthy fertility and pregnancy.

If you are on this prayer journey in preparation for parenthood, consider the circumstances that may challenge your faith to hope for a future generation. Should personal circumstances present challenges for pregnancy, this is the phase to redeem any worldly mindset.

Unlock Godly Purpose

Consider the biological role-players involved in this future generation, keeping in mind those relevant to the person you are praying for. What were the tendencies of both sets of parents and past family lines? (Tendencies are those default choice of behaviours in similar circumstances.)

Consider these tendencies, as well as any recurring incidents such as:

- Marital or relational problems (including divorce, unfaithfulness, promiscuity, pornography, staying unmarried)
- All types of abuse (verbal, emotional, financial, sexual and physical) towards a marriage partner, children, family, employees or others (including other religions or cultures)
- Having children outside out of wedlock
- Emotional struggles such as depression or anxiety, irrational behaviours, lack of emotional control, anger, bitterness and unforgiveness, hatred towards other cultures/religions/groups/family members

- Behavioural issues in careers, including unhealthy pressure to succeed or a lack of motivation and drive
- Self-rejection, inferiority, shame, self-loathing, self-harming, suicide
- Poverty or regular failures in life or an unhealthy love of money
- Abortions
- Miscarriages

If miscarriages or abortions previously occurred with the mother of the loved one you are praying for, these may still have an impact on the body in the womb, as well as in the production and functioning of reproductive organs.

In the case of miscarriages or abortions, it may be necessary to pray over the loss, shock and grieving that comes with that, as well as any guilt involved due to these experiences. Through such occurrences, death has entered the womb – the original place of life. This needs to be addressed and life invited back into the "cradle of life".

Due to the human choice regarding abortions – rejecting the truth that God is the giver of life – it will be necessary to bring this choice before God and ask His forgiveness.[1]

In some cases, twins were conceived originally, but one passed away prior to birth or during early pregnancy. If you are aware of this, pray over that loss, death and the cleansing of the womb (before the one for who you are praying was conceived). Also pray over the bond between the twins – the one living and the one who passed. Should the surviving twin battle with a sense of guilt (with or without understanding why), pray over the guilt and loss and the possible fruit of depression. Ask Father God to restore his right to live and enjoy life to the full.

- Sicknesses and other physical ailments or shortcomings that occurred in family lineages
- Negative words spoken over having children (don't want to have children due to preference, lifestyle or distrust in state of the world), wanting "only one child", or "no more children", i.e. rejecting any additional pregnancies (children) as unwanted
- Desiring only a specific gender in your offspring

With adopted children or stepchildren, both the biological and the adopted or step-parent's lives have to be considered: the behavioural and emotional tendencies, habits, struggles – spiritually, emotionally and physically.

Do you recognise the traits and tendencies of the relevant generations? You can bring the negative ones before God and ask Him to break those generational tendencies and cleanse the data transferred from generation to generation. We will discuss the principles of epigenetics in the following sessions.

Bring harmful words before God and ask Him to free your loved one from the negative, limiting and rejecting impact and message over his life.

These may include:

- "I can't afford/don't want another pregnancy now . . ."
- "I don't want to bring more children/another child into this world . . ."
- "'I so wanted a girl, not a boy . . .", etc.

Declare truth over your loved one, "You are welcome and planned by Him – the only Source of life. You are exactly who you should be!"

This is not a season for spending months and years on delving into bloodlines. It merely deals with the aspects at hand and brings ungodly and disrespectful details before Him and then asks Father God, your Re-Creator to *cleanse and renew* the message of this phase's events to be in unity and agreement with Him.

Consider the *circumstances* prior to conception:

- Trauma such as accidents, attacks or abuse can impact the sense of security. Were the circumstances prior to conception safe? Calm? Financially secure? Physically secure? Emotionally secure?
- What were the environmental circumstances during this phase of your loved one? Was there famine, starvation, pandemics, drought or other natural disasters? Was the country where he was born involved in war?

Pray over the impact on the relevant individual and for the restoration of calmness, as well as for your loved one to have healthy sense of security and safety. This will form an important part in developing a robust self-confidence in his ability to cope with life.

Trauma can be transferred from generation to generation.[2]

How did this phase act as a foundation for your loved one's sense of self? If you are his mother, what was your experience and understanding of who you are? And that of the father?

Remember: In the rhythm of prayer, you cancel the negative declarations and establish the godly Truth over your loved one.

This journey is not only a cleansing of what should *not* be part of your loved one's life, but also a filling-up of what *should* be part of his life, i.e. a realignment of what He says over him and a restoration of his inheritance in Jesus.

Declare His Word over your loved one. The Word is not to be used as some form of magic, but when declared from a heart conviction and from relationship with Him, it recreates and renews as the Word realigns with truth.

Ask, "What is the relevant and attention-worthy information that happened before my loved one came into being? What have I heard or picked up just listening to general chats during family gatherings that might play a role in his battle with this or that, or behaving in such and such a manner?"

May this be a process of reconsolidation of your loved ones' memories. It can change to such an extent that the structure of the neural connections adapts to the new, physically measurable version![3]

The physical always manifests the spiritual. Take heart, and be encouraged so that your faith can rise to the level of change required in this time and season.

Prayer for Phase 1

Thank you, our Lord and King, for moving effortlessly to and fro in time.

Thank you, Father, that You are a timeless God and our Re-Creator. You renew and redeem!

Thank you, Father, that I am safe in Your light. I welcome Your light of revelation and truth. You are God Emmanuel, God with me! Thank you that You journey with me.

I ask you now to move back in time to redeem the history of _____.

I ask forgiveness for negative words spoken regarding pregnancy, having children or being a parent. Please render the negative words null and void over _____.

I now declare that the future of _____ is filled with hope, acceptance and love, even prior to _____ being conceived.

I ask You, my Father God, to protect me and every one of my loved ones who form part of this journey. Please protect me from being overwhelmed with information or being intimidated with specifics and terminologies with which I am not familiar. I will embark on this phase with confidence in You.

Please protect me from the clutter of information and feelings of being judged or burdened. Remove this from me in Jesus' Name as I bring all relevant and revealed sin (my own and those of my predecessors) before You and receive Your forgiveness. I am redeemed by Your Blood, Lord Jesus, and stand with new boldness before Your Throne of Grace as I journey.

Thank you that as I am not able to move back in time, You are. Therefore, my Father, I ask that You recreate and realign the history of my loved one to restore his perception of who You are, who he is and what life is all about.

Will You please restore any state of disregard, rejection or physical and spiritual unhealthiness of _____ in the pre-conception period? Redeem this atmosphere to one of knowing he is loved, appreciated, celebrated and safe on every level.

Father, will You transform the environment of Phase 1 from fear (of rejection, shame, failure, disappointment and humiliation) to love? Love accepts unconditionally. It is kind and safe and celebrates the space of being the original person You created.

May the reality of Your involvement in our lives overrule every thought and perception that denies this truth. May I and _____ become increasingly more aware of Your commitment to us, longing to reunite us and restore the love bonds from heart to heart.

You are our safe space; You are our Redeemer. Thank you, Father!

We honour and love You!

I ask with boldness in Jesus' Name. Amen.

KEY SCRIPTURES	
Ephesians 4:24	Psalm 34:13
Colossians 3:10	Psalm 35:28
Romans 4:7	Psalm 51:14
Nehemiah 9:2	Proverbs 15:4
Psalm 103:3	Psalm 139:4
Isaiah 53:5	Proverbs 12:18
James 3:5, 6, 8	1 Peter 3:10

1. Van den Berg, G. *A Change of Heart*, pp. 204–226. 1st edition. South Africa: Suiderkruis Boeke.
2. *Can the Legacy of Trauma Be Passed Down the Generations?* http://www.bbc.com/future/story/20190326-what-is-epigenetics.
3. Dahlitz, M. 2017. *The Psychotherapist's Essential Guide to the Brain*. Brisbane, Australia.

✏️ Notes

Phase 2: Conception

REDEEMED DNA

I was found before I was lost.

I was loved before I was known.

The joy of *knowing* someone holds various layers of understanding. Knowing includes being aware of the other person's character, who they are, including gifts and flaws, joys and frustrations. To love the other because of these, not in spite of, is to celebrate their humanity.

To be known as such is a joy and a part of your Father's blessing. Knowing Father God and *being* known by Him should be your primal heart's cry, the way Moses declared in Exodus 33:13, AMP:

> *"Now therefore, I pray you, if I have found favour in Your sight, let me know Your ways so that I may know You."*

The Hebrew word for "know" in this verse is *yada,* holding the meaning of a process to gain insight and new conviction.

Paraphrased, the verse above may read as follows: *May I gradually become more deeply and intimately acquainted with who You are by focusing on You, acknowledging You and understanding You better.*

May you be like Moses in seeking to know Him!

Knowing is a process. It includes growing in understanding and changing accordingly. According to the Suzuki Violin School's method of learning[1], the path of knowing is through:

1. Listening
2. Imitation
3. Repetition.

Knowing starts with hearing.

The *shema* (declaration of faith) is a proclamation calling Israel (and you as a believer) to *hear*. Deuteronomy 6:4, AMP, says, *"Hear, O Israel! The LORD is our God, the LORD is one [the only God]!"*.

To hear is to listen with intent.

Hearing brings understanding.
Understanding brings insight.
Insight brings change – in thought, behaviour and relationships.

To know and be known as in the Hebrew sense of *yada* entails a deep walk of gaining trust and therefore a capacity to invite the other person into your innermost space. Such a bond of trust and commitment is a covenant. This is what intimacy is all about. This is where conception of another human should occur.

Outside of such a securely loving environment, the firewall of protection is hacked, and harmful invasions may transpire. Come and journey into Phase 2.

The Secret Library

Conception is a process, and fertilisation is part of it. This incredibly complex process reveals the magnificence of your Creator.

The science writer Michael Banks, from Bristol in the United Kingdom, explains the fascinating biology, chemistry and physics involved during fertilisation. The mere shape of the sperm cell's head and tail, which effectively enables it to reach the desired destination, is deserving of our highest applause! [2]

After fertilisation, the egg cell must move back to the ovum for binding and development. A new life begins. *Spora,* the Greek word for seed, which includes the parenting seed, consists of the egg cell that is fertilised by the sperm cell. This seed contains genetic data regarding generational codes, hereditary trademarks, tendencies and abilities – all filled with massive potential!

All the genetic information from both biological parents is merged during fertilisation. This is referred to as the *genome*. It consists of DNA molecules made up of two double helix strings with a total volume[2] per string pair of a miniscule three billionth cubic mm (3×10^{-9} mm^3). There are different types of DNA – some for protein production and some for other purposes. The inherited data is carried and communicated in these tiny containers. The genome would be like a library, the chromosomes the books, and the gene the chapters.[3]

The most intriguing organelles involved in this fascinating event are the mitochondria. They are tiny organelles operating as the power station of the cell. In this phase, it is worth mentioning that the mitochondria are the only organelles that contain their own DNA, and are called the mitochondrial DNA. This genetic information is inherited from the mother's DNA. The mitochondria in sperm are found in the sperm's tail, which falls off at fertilisation. This special DNA is therefore referred to as the Mitochondrial Eve, the matrilineal most recent common ancestor (MRCA) of all human beings.[4]

These organelles also determine cell apoptosis – cell suicide – or the death of cells. If the mitochondria do not function properly, the chance of tumours growing might increase. The healthy activity of these organelles also supports strong focus ability and energy.

Keep this in mind as you pray through the keynotes in this phase.

Your loved ones' stories are transferred from generation to generation. Within every generation, new stories are added. Stories are embedded in the new being – the embryo.

> Your inherited data does not define you. You are not only the product of your parents' DNA.

Does this mean that you and your child are simply subjected to your generational history? Does this leave you helpless, like victims of the past?

Definitely not!

The concept of epigenetics supports this statement in a psychological and biological way. *Epi* means "in addition", and *genetics* is the word used to describe your inherited data. Your inherited data, therefore, does not define you. You, your children, your spouse and other loved ones are not only the product of your parents' DNA.

This field of study was first explored as a concept in 1942 by embryologist, Conrad Waddington, and later was given more attention by Ernst Hadorn. Ongoing research was done on the impact on various areas of human development, medication, social, and emotional health. The study field largely demonstrates how change becomes not only possible, but visible and measurable. Change is constant and a constant reality.[5][6]

Epigenetics is the field of study of how environmental and experiential stimuli can be accommodated by your genetic adaptation. It does not include changes in the DNA sequence or structure, but in the genetic *expression,* which eventually manifests in measurable change, for example, a change in metabolism with long-term diet and exercise.

In other words, the environment or the specific experiences may cause adaptational change in the phenotype without changing the genotype, the genetic data of a person. *Phenotype* is the visible characteristics or trademarks in a person due to the interactions between the genotype and the environment, i.e. the phenotype makes the genotype's expression visible and measurable in behaviour.

This is significantly true regarding your habits and tendencies – you no longer have the excuse of blaming the fathers' short fuse or the mother's stubbornness.

Every person begins life with the right to choose what their response would be to the primal question, *Who am I?* Each one of us is a unique product of our Creator God; you are His choice because you carry His breath of life.

John 1:1–4, KJV, states:

> *In the beginning was the Word, and the Word was with God, and the Word was God. The same was in the beginning with God. All things were made by him; and without him was not anything made that was made. In him was life; and the life was the light of men.*

This is also affirmed in Genesis 1:26–28, KJV:

> *And God said, Let us make man in our image, after our likeness: and let them have dominion over the fish of the sea, and over the fowl of the air, and over the cattle, and over all the earth, and over every creeping thing that creepeth upon the earth. So God created man in his own image, in the image of God created he him; male and female created he them. And God blessed them, and God said unto them, Be fruitful, and multiply, and replenish the earth, and subdue it: and have dominion . . .*

The Message Translation (MSG) states, ". . . make them reflecting our nature . . .", instead of ". . . in the image of God. . .". The theme of Phase 2 is "Redeemed DNA".

He alone is the Source of Life. Why does He breathe His breath of life into you? Why does He give you the gift of life? Primarily in order for you to have a personal relationship with Him, to know Him and to find your home in His presence.

On a secondary scale, your calling is to serve Him with your uniqueness and, as co-servers in the Kingdom, to reconcile others to Him.

But all these things are from God, who reconciled us to Himself through Christ [making us acceptable to Him] and gave us the ministry of reconciliation [so that by our example we might bring others to Him], that is, that God was in Christ reconciling the world to Himself, not counting people's sins against them [but canceling them]. And He has committed to us the message of reconciliation [that is, restoration to favor with God].

– 2 CORINTHIANS 5:18–19, AMP

If you battle to believe this, this essential truth might also slip through your children's fingers. Their inherited data and experiential interpretations might continue to be you and your loved one's "truth" – a potentially distorted truth version, and therefore not the truth at all.

You are treasured by your Father God. His love has claimed you and He enjoys the right of *first claim* over you. This is a spiritual law in which you can trust.

. . . just as [in His love] He chose us in Christ [actually selected us for Himself as His own] before the foundation of the world, so that we would be holy [that is, consecrated, set apart for Him, purpose-driven] and blameless in His sight. In love He predestined and lovingly planned for us to be adopted to Himself as [His own] children through Jesus Christ, in accordance with the kind intention and good pleasure of His will.

– EPHESIANS 1:4–5, AMP

🔑 Keys

The time of conception should preferably occur within the context of respectful love and the celebration of life.

When generational prayer altars have been burning regularly due to continual intercession and declarations of blessings, a powerful spiritual space has been prepared for the new and coming generations. This is ideal. Parents who are surrendered to God will understand how to speak blessings over the growing and coming generations, as well as to recall and reclaim the blessings of the past.

A prayer altar consists of rhythms of prayer and intercession for similar topics, for example for family and loved ones, for your country or specific countries, etc., not letting go of your heart cry before His Throne of Grace. Remember that God is your Father, but He is also your King and your Judge. Pursue knowing Him in all of these positions.

Sadly, conception can also occur within a manipulative and disrespectful environment, leaving the little victim to fight for survival on an emotional, spiritual and often physical level as well.

The physical and emotional environment during conception creates the atmosphere in which the new life develops. These first moments when the fertilised egg is attached and starts to multiply are holy and filled with the very breath of God. It is therefore important to take note of what the environment was like when your loved one was conceived.

This is walking back for a better future, and changing the impact of your loved one's history. History can be rewritten and redeemed: the negative, damaging impact's expansion or build-up is stopped and a brand-new restoration sphere is being installed. Trust Father God to rewrite this history – to redeem the impact.

David cried out to God, "GOD rewrote the text of my life when I opened the book of my heart to his eyes" (Psalm 18:24, MSG).

Therefore, your journey IS prayer-worthy!

As you journey through each phase, you will be confronted with your own past. Make use of every opportunity as it surfaces. These little pieces of gold are packed with growth potential as you invite and welcome Father God and His Spirit to bring light and life (see John 1:4–5). This includes the beautiful and the ugly stuff of the past – both are potentially good and potentially bad (for example, if you had a very sheltered upbringing, you might be more inclined to expect that kind of treatment throughout your life).

Bring this conception phase of your loved one before Father's Throne of Grace:

- Was it safely inside the marriage covenant?
- Was lust or sexual perversion part of this process?
- Was it during a time of financial worries or other worrisome burdens?
- Was there disrespect, dominance or control, force, manipulation or intimidation involved?
- Was it part of family planning or an unexpected blessing/burden?

Pray over these aspects where applicable and forgive those who need to be forgiven (not from a viewpoint of deserving it, but only by grace). Pray for the restoration of distorted identities, and a realignment to His truth regarding:

1. Who you are.
2. Your loved one is.
3. Others are.
4. God is; and
5. Life is.

These phases position you in how you approach life, and how you cope with the various challenges that come naturally while doing life.

The primary question of the heart is, *Who am I?* Your self-definition is formed from pre-conception. It forms your story and is part of your history. Therefore, pray through this phase with great care to bring your loved one's story into alignment with His Story.

A huge part of this heart question concerns the right to be alive, to be here on planet Earth. Do you have this right? Does your loved one have this right?

Yes, definitely!

You carry incredible value in your uniqueness. A Professor in Science and Conception and Chairman of the Genesis-research Trust, Lord Robert Winston, made the following statement, "My parents would have to have another 1 x 10 to the power of 15 babies to have a child with the same genes as mine." It is therefore safe to say there will never be another "you" on this planet.[7]

You are beautiful in your complexity and every piece of this phase of conception leaves us in awe and wonder of our super-creative God! It makes this phase supremely prayer-worthy.

Everyone has an invisible document – your Birthright, given to you as He breathes His breath of life into you.

Your birthright includes:

Your right to be born and to live.
Your right to know the Truth, to know Jesus, your Salvation.
Your right to choose. The power of choice is man's superpower – use it well.

We will discuss this document in more detail in the next phase. Ask Father God to reconcile this invisible document with your loved one and all it includes.

In Deuteronomy 21:17, the Word speaks of the *birthright* of Esau – the right of the first-born to have a position as first heir and leader of the family next to the father, as well as inheriting a double portion of his father's estate.

Please note: This birthright has to do with *position* and *inheritance*.

Jesus is God, the Father's firstborn Son, and you are a redeemed of the Lord, through your faith in the redemptive work of Jesus, the firstborn. Where does that leave you and your family?

According to the message of Romans 8:16–17, you are a co-heir with Him and may gratefully enjoy the privileges thereof. You have this *redeemed* birthright with a *redeemed* position and a *redeemed* inheritance.

You are reborn from the immortal seed (*spora*) of the living God!

KEY SCRIPTURES	
2 Corinthians 5:15–17	Romans 8:14–19
1 John 3:1–2	Ecclesiastes 3:11

Seed Carries Inheritance!

What does this inheritance mean for you and your loved ones?

You, as the intercessor for your loved ones, can now come before the Throne of Grace and pray that your inherited genetic data (your genes from the egg and sperm cell) will be aligned with this truth. Ask that your loved ones will be renewed according to His redemptive work, so that any distorted identity and concept of who the Father is and who you are will be restored to His truth.

You may gratefully join Him, being your Father's Firstborn Son.

As reborn children of the Almighty, you carry godly genetic codes in your DNA. What a joy to know you are reborn as a co-heir with His DNA's codes and abilities! Keep the principle of epigenetics in mind as you journey through this phase, and gain guidelines on how to align your child's genetic tendencies to His.

Ask Father God for Holy Spirit-implemented recreation of your loved ones' genetic codes or markers as renewed characteristics – in line with who they were supposed to be, their original selves.

The godly tendencies and qualities that you need to pray for in your children, for them to have, enjoy and manifest, are:

- Hope
- Faith
- Discernment
- Joy
- Hunger for Truth
- Eagerness towards Him and being in His presence
- Increasing capacity for His presence and truth
- The desire to know Him
- A Kingdom and reigning mindset/mentality
- A victorious approach to life
- Godly resilience – spiritually, mentally, physically and emotionally
- A heart attitude that will influence and lead/inspire/impact

- Healthy self-respect and love
- Knowing their calling and life purpose

Pray that godly markers (DNA) will be activated in your loved ones' lives – for the purpose of entering and enjoying their sole purpose and calling, and that the redeemed's identity will be established and will function.

Pray also that their self-definition – the Who am I? *question of the heart – will be Father God's definition, and that it will settle and be engraved on the tablets of their hearts.*

Prayer for Phase 2

An amazing thought to consider is that our Father, who knew us individually, completely, long before He formed us, is the same Engineer who knew every minute detail of our being as we grew mystically in the secret sanctuary of our mother's womb! And He knows us now, and longs to introduce us to ourselves again, so that we may know, even as we have always been known! (see Jeremiah 1:5; 1 Corinthians 13:12, *Mirror Bible*)

Our Father God, You are the Creator and Life-giver!

Thank you for breathing the breath of life into me during me and _____'s conception.

Thank you for giving me and _____ 's birthright. We may know You, the Author and Finisher of our lives.

My heart is in awe of how You love _____ and have engineered his life, his uniqueness and his future. You have had _____ in Your heart all along. You are an incredible God and Creator!

Father God, I now bring _____ before Your Throne of Grace and ask You to redeem his birthright into alignment with Your will and his true calling and purpose in life. May he know You and find his home in Your Presence.

Thank you, Father God, for restoring _____'s godly position and inheritance.

Please activate the godly codes of _____'s DNA so that his self-definition will be healthy and functional according to his original self (who You called him to be). May it settle in his heart.

Father, will Your Holy Spirit now come and implement the recreation of _____'s genetic codes to facilitate _____'s full potential.

I ask You now to activate the potential encoding of the following in _____'s life: hope, faith, discernment, wisdom, joy, a hunger for truth and a capacity accordingly, a desire to know (yada) You, just as Moses desired You, a kingdom mindset, a victorious approach to life, godly resilience, a heart attitude to influence and lead, a healthy self-regard and love, knowing, being aligned to and pursuing his calling and life purpose.

Thank you, my Father, for Your love and grace to recreate.

I love You and honour You.

In Jesus' Name I pray. Amen.

KEY SCRIPTURES	
Jeremiah 1:5	John 1:4–5
John 1:1–4	Deuteronomy 21:17
Genesis 1:26–31	Romans 8:17
2 Corinthians 5:17–18	1 John 3:1

1. *The Suzuki Method*. https://www3.uwsp.edu.
2. Banks, M. 2022. *The Secret Science of Baby*. Dallas: BenBella Books. ISBN: 9781637741467.
3. Gitt, W. 1999. *The Wonder of Man*. Bieleveld: Christeliche LiteraturVerbreitung. ISBN: 9783893973972.
4. *Mitochondrial Eve*. ISOGG - International Society of Genetic Genealogy 2004. https://www.virginia.edu/woodson/courses/ aas102%20(spring%2001)/articles/tierney.html. Newsweek 111; Jan 11, 1988. *Mitochondrial Eve*. Wikipedia. https://en.wikipedia.org.
5. Dahlitz, M. 2017. *The Psychotherapist's Essential Guide to the Brain*. Brisbane, Australia. www.whatisepigenetics.com.
6. Mauritzio M. 2014. *The Social Brain Meets the Reactive Genome: Neuroscience, Epigenetics and the New Social Biology*. Hypothesis and Theory Article. School of Sociology and Social Policy. Institute for Science and Society, University of Nottingham, UK. Human Neuroscience.
7. Winston, R. 2004. 1st edition. *What Makes Me Me?* NY: DK Children.

Notes

Phase 3:
In the Womb

BONDING

Now this is what YAHWEH says, "Listen, Jacob, to the One who created you, Israel, to the one who shaped who you are. Do not fear, for I, your Kinsman Redeemer, will rescue you. I have called you by your name, and you are mine."

— ISAIAH 43:1, TPT

You are loved.
You are welcome.
You are safe.
You are pursued.
Your King wants to know you.

Choosing Life

A reward is something good that you receive with merit. But the Father of all creation rewards you due to *His* merit. You and I are the receivers of a dependant human being because of His grace and because He loves to spoil His children with undeserved rewards such as . . . children.

Behold, children are a heritage and gift from the Lord, the fruit of the womb a reward.

— PSALM 127:3, AMP

For You formed my innermost parts; You knit me [together] in my mother's womb.

– PSALM 139:13, AMP

From the moment your heart starts beating, you are turned toward life! At four weeks, the cells that form the heart have gathered. At week five, this group of cells, soon to be the heart, starts pumping. At six weeks, the embryonic cells beat 110 times per minute. The agreement with the Giver of Life is in action![12]

In the light of the previous two phases, the tiny new human now has a physical status and is a living, breathing creature, a soul, and will continue throughout his earthly life within this physical body.

According to Scripture, man:

- Was created by God – in His likeness, male and female (see Genesis 1:27)
- Was created as a body from the dust of the ground (see Genesis 2:7)
- Received his spirit through the living energy of God's divine breath, the Spirit of Life (see Genesis 2:7). (Breath of life: *neshamah* – wind, energy, divine inspiration, intellect.)
- Became a living being, a soul (Hebrew: *nephesh*), as God breathed life into his physical body (see Genesis 2:7; 1 Corinthians 15:45–49)

But life can only come from life, and the living God is the only self-existent Being, so it must ultimately come from Him. It was only to man that God directly (rather than from a distance, as it were, by His spoken Word) "breathed" in the "breath of life".

– HENRY MORRIS[3]

In Scripture, the three Greek words used for "life" are:

1. *zõé* – eternal, divine life (see John 10:10)
2. *bíos* – physical life (see Luke 8:14)
3. *psychē* – soul life, immortal soul, a living, breathing creature, spirit (see Matthew 16:25).

You do not *have* a soul; you *are* a soul.[4] You and your loved ones are created to love the Lord your God with all your heart, all your mind and with all your will, to love Him with your entire soul!

The physical version of the dream that your Creator God had in His heart finally manifests. This new human reveals the heart of an adoring Father and triggers the parental calling of those entrusted with him.

The question that we must now ask is: *Will the ears of the father and mother hear what the Spirit of Creator God is asking and declaring over this new child?*

The Power of First Experiences

The Womb phase is an initiation time – an incredible time of development on all levels: physical (visible) and spiritual (invisible). It is a time of growing and forming bonds. The theme of Phase 3 is "Bonding".

During this phase, the nerve cells reach a staggering amount of close to 86 billion and can grow by up to 100 000 per minute. If you study embryonic development, you will want to continually sing praise songs as it is the most incredible visible work of art and the most astonishing miracle (other than rebirth and godly transformation).

A brief look at the developmental correlations between cognitive and emotional development is necessary as you journey through this phase.

It is a season of bonding. Whatever bonds are formed in the womb will initiate future bonding baselines. The primary bond formed between the new human and the biological mother is referred to as Maternal Foetal Attachment (MFA). It is the bond between the foetus and the biological mother in whose womb he is developing.

Janet DiPietro, a developmental psychologist at the Johns Hopkins University, USA, states that the socio-emotional regulation starts during the foetal period, with the focus on the 20–28th weeks.[5]

This synchronisation between the mother's and the foetus' emotional states are strong indicators of future emotional, physical, social and spiritual capacities by both parties.

Marilyn Lewis, in her study on the relationship of maternal foetal bonding in a subsequent pregnancy, stated, "Maternal foetal bonding is the emotional investment a woman has for her foetus and is the foundation for nurturing and protection." [6]

Studies show:

- *A weak MFA* contributes to potentially lower cognitive and social abilities in the foetus, as well as lower empathy in both mother and baby.
- The foetus may battle with emotional management (congruency) and effective self-regulation, i.e. he might battle to develop a healthy regard of self.

The heart's primary question is, "Who am I?" [7]

This core question guides our search for the meaning of life and who to bond with. Social impact influences this definition and leaves the foetus dependent on unconditional acceptance and love by the mother – the biological human in whose womb he is growing.

A typical question might be, *If the primary human in your life does not accept and love you unconditionally, who will?*

Consider the question of the relevant loved one: *Was I loved and welcomed after the awareness of pregnancy?* Any hesitance or negative response will indicate a level of rejection and result in trauma.

Trauma during this phase can contribute to a weak MFA. Therefore, ask these questions: *Was there any shame regarding the pregnancy of my loved one? What were the circumstances? Was it secure and emotionally safe?*

Studies by the American Psychological Association in 2020 have shown that a high occurrence of serious conflict during pregnancy has a direct impact on birth risk with regard to birth weight, early term/pre-term and APGAR count. Please consider:

- Was the mother happy about the pregnancy, the timing of it and the gender of the baby?
- How was the mother supported during this phase?
- How was the mother's self-image and self-respect?
- Did the mother or the foetus suffer any complications or health issues during the pregnancy?

Keep in mind that a foetus has the physical ability to form memories and to remember from:

1. 30 weeks – recall 10 minutes later;
2. 34 weeks – recall up to 4 weeks later.

A strong MFA contributes to healthy family environments and has a positive impact on foetus development and the birth process, as well as the adaptation of both the mother and baby post-birth.

The mother has . . .

- a healthier state during pregnancy.
- the ability to adapt to her new role as mother with a healthy instinct.
- protection against postnatal depression.

The foetus has . . .

- stronger emotional congruency.
- the ability to self-sooth.
- stronger emotional resilience.

- healthy empathy.
- healthy social bonds.
- higher cognitive capacity.

These are the building blocks to trust. Trust supports faith . . . hopefully in God.

> The state of the MFA determines the womb's atmosphere!

As stated before: The primary (first) bond will initiate the new individual's default attachment bond — with others, with God and with themselves.

The Two Types of Bonds

There are mainly two types of bonds involved with the MFA. Because it is the first bond formed between the foetus and another, it will operate as the default or baseline bond within these primary areas of bonding — other people, God and ourselves. We also bond with the environment.

You either form primary love bonds or primary fear bonds. As you journey through the phases, you will look at what role these two bonding types play on you and your loved ones' lives. This baseline bonding influences your approach to life in general, your choices and your relationships. For the purposes of this journey, consider the following:

- A low MFA will indicate the main bonding type as fear bonds.
- A high (healthy) MFA will indicate the main bonding type as love bonds.
- A low MFA may indicate low self-definition or a distorted answer to "Who am I?"
- A strong (healthy) MFA may indicate a healthier/stable definition of "Who am I?"

Spirit to spirit

A mother's spiritual state has a direct impact on the foetus' spiritual growth state. A healthy spiritual state will include a secure self-regard according to what the Creator God intended. Our Creator made man and said, "God saw everything that He had made, and behold, it was *very* good and He validated it completely" (Genesis 1:31, AMP, author emphasis added).

Man and all creation are God's delight! It was man alone who was made in His likeness and it was to man that He gave complete authority over His creation (see Genesis 1:26).

Elohim (the Most High God) chose to appoint man to govern the earth and to enjoy the beauty of His creation. Above all, He desired for man *to know Him* and to be loved and to feel validated in His love. The love of your Creator Father draws you to His presence and realigns you with His Truth.

A sound understanding that you are loved and that your life matters provides a healthy capacity to receive the Father's love and counsel, and to love and care for others in a healthy and effective manner. What you think of yourself, and how you talk about yourself indicates what your current state of self-regard is. Respect and love can never be separated.

Keep in mind that a distorted image of yourself can limit your faith and confidence in the love that your Creator God has for you. It can produce insecurity and a co-dependant approach in relationships. A distorted self-image may include both extremes of the spectrum, ranging from a narcissistic self-centredness to a dangerously low sense of self-worth, disregarding the truth that your life matters. The manner of attachment to self, others and God can become twisted. Malfunctioning in the various areas in your life (or your loved one's life) can result from this.

The Cord of Love
The physical often manifests the spiritual.

During this phase, the umbilical cord is the main transporter of nutrients from the primary source to the dependant.

Pray that in a similar manner, Father God, as your main Source, will provide you and your family with all you need to grow and thrive into the people you are supposed to be. Provision will include *spiritual* nutrients such as life, love, truth, health, peace, faith, strength, joy, etc.

Cords and bonds connect one person with another and one being with another, heart to heart. Eventually the spiritual umbilical cord will operate as a highway, secure and thriving in provision. It carries non-verbal messages between the two destinations, such as love, encouragement, blessings and confidence.

Pray that the cord (bond) between mother and foetus be one of unconditional love and will carry a "you matter"- message.

Essential nutrients are provided through the umbilical cord and so also through the invisible cord – providing the basic needs (emotional and spiritual) that every human requires. These are the building blocks for self-definition.

⚷ Unlocking Identity
A golden key for prayer would be: Pray that the Truth message will be safely carried to your loved one's heart – you are loved, safe and welcome!

This is the primal desire of the heart, to secure the foundation for a healthy and godly identity – your unique heart print.

Who am I, the question of the heart, includes *Am I welcome? Am I loved? Am I safe? Am I who I am supposed to be?* Identity includes physical appearance (build, height, eye colour, etc.), gender identity, personality and abilities . . . (remember Phase 2).

Pray that any distortion, deception or confusion of the abovementioned will be rectified and that the truth regarding your loved one's identity will be restored to its original state (as Created by Father God).

> A healthy respect for life will turn the person towards everything that aligns with life.

Pray that the invisible spiritual "umbilical" cords will be restored to love cords (bonds) and that your loved one will be nourished with all the spiritual nutrients he was supposed to receive during this phase.

When the new little being is safely connected to his mother, his whole being will turn towards life! He will choose life! This is a vital position to have for the rest of his life — and might be his default approach to the situations and challenges that life will bring. Choosing life or being love-orientated allows him to make the most of opportunities, and for his original identity to fully develop and celebrate his uniqueness.

Positive love bonds during this phase may orientate your little one towards healthy bonds with others, himself and with Father God. He will have a natural regard for life and all it offers, a natural baseline to cope with the necessary emotional and cognitive capacity.

A healthy respect for life will turn the person towards everything that aligns with life. This will include safe friendships, a healthy exploration and investigation of all life has to offer, as well as a hunger for the Word of God. The living Word is the Bread of Life (see John 6:33; 35; 48–51).

Pray that there will be a hunger for the Bread of Life and a discernment for substandard bread. Speak life and blessings over physical development, emotional health (joy), cognitive maturation and spiritual discernment, with peace as the gatekeeper of the heart.

The Brain and Attachment

Acknowledged role-players in the study field of MFA are the British psychologist John Bowlby and American psychologist and researcher in neuropsychology, Dr Allan Schore. Both their studies show how the right brain is involved in forming the first (primal) bonds or attachments. The right brain develops and matures first. The left brain will develop further in the first two years after birth.

All attachment experiences are stored in the right brain, which has more bonds with the rest of the body, the Central Nervous System and the HPA-axis (Hypothalamic-pituitary-adrenal axis). The HPA-axis plays an enormous role in handling stress and the restoration from stressful experiences, and will be discussed in more detail later.

The development of emotional love bonds with the foetus is therefore the primary role-player in how the young human will eventually react to stressful situations (impacting effective emotional regulation). Neuro-behavioural development seems to be directly impacted by pre-birth stress in the foetus.[8]

DiPietro's research (mentioned earlier) further shows that adverse birth phenotype and foetal exposure to maternal stress (emotional and biological) shows a high risk for cognitive disorders and changes in brain structures.

Pray for the full restoration and development of the right brain regarding bonds and trauma. During this phase, forgive where applicable and pray over the nervous system and the developmental vulnerabilities due to trauma.

Trauma includes destructive experiences, as well as the absence of basic needs. This will be discussed in more detail in the next phases.

According to Dr J Lee Nelson, there is an incredible exchange between the cells of the foetus and the mother. The foetus' cells circulate through the mother's body to various areas — including the brain, where it can move through the blood-brain barrier to become neurones. They can, for example, also move to the liver to become liver cells.[9]

This vast exchange of cells supports healing in the mother's and the baby's bodies, even long after giving birth, both being impacted by their unique DNA.

Some of the foetus' cells protect the mother from certain illnesses. How or whether this has an impact on autoimmune diseases are also being investigated. How much more will this interconnectedness bless both individuals on invisible levels!

Looking at the connection between Elizabeth's foetus, John, and his nephew, Jesus, when Mary entered the room provides biblical evidence for the ability of a foetus to sense and respond on a spiritual level, as well as on a physical one. John leaped in his mother's womb when he sensed the presence of the King of kings and his mother was filled with the Holy Spirit!

> *Now at this time Mary arose and hurried to the hill country, to a city of Judah (Judea), and she entered the house of Zacharias and greeted Elizabeth. When Elizabeth heard Mary's greeting, her baby leaped in her womb; and Elizabeth was filled with the Holy Spirit and empowered by Him.*
>
> — LUKE 1:39–41, AMP

Pray that this exchanged impact will bless and work for the good in your loved one's life, as well as for His glory!

Birthright

If there was any attempt to abort the foetus or any womb deaths during or prior to this child's womb phase, pray that his birthright will be secured or restored. The consequences of these deaths can manifest in various areas of your loved one's life, for example, depression, restlessness (wandering), a feeling of not belonging or having the right to be here (imposter syndrome), anger, pushing people away, being apathetic, and having a procrastinating approach to life.

Pray over these signs or consequences of death by asking Father God to breath His life into these areas. Pray that the vital attachments will be restored with the primary source of love and comfort: your Father God and His Holy Spirit. Pray that these bonds will restore and equip your loved ones with the capacity and ability to be who they were originally created to be.

The heart with its primary question, "Who am I?", longs to know that your life matters, that you are meant be here and that you have worth and significance.

Pray that the message of being unconditionally loved, of being welcome and safe will be engraved on the tablets of your loved one's heart.

The foetus' presence, physical, emotional and spiritual development, appearance and gender are His choice. Declare it over them that they are accepted and celebrated. Father God's creation of your loved one must be blessed!

Prayer for Phase 3

My wonderful Creator God, thank you that You wove myself and my loved ones so delicately together in the womb.

Your Word says even the darkness hides nothing from You! Thank you that my loved one was delicately knit together in the womb and his inward parts were formed by You during this phase. (see Psalm 139:12–13)

Thank you, Father, that Your Word says that my loved one's frame was not hidden from You when he was being formed in secret and intricately and curiously wrought [as if embroidered with various colours] in the depths of the earth. Your eyes saw our unformed substance and in Your book all the days of our lives were written before they even took shape.

You are a magnificent Father and I honour and worship You, Creator God.

Thank you that I can bring _____ to You today and present my heart's desires regarding his time in the womb before Your Throne of Grace.

Father, please restore the primary bond between me (the mother) and _____, even from as far back as during being pregnant with _____.

Please will You transform every fear bond into a love bond – where _____ may feel unconditionally loved and celebrated in his beautiful uniqueness.

Restore any distorted perception on his identity (including gender, personality, name received, abilities and physical self). Realign these aspects with Your original plan and purpose for _____.

My precious Father, please will You restore all distorted or hurtful attachment memories stored away in _____'s right brain and reconsolidate them with the Truth regarding Your love and acceptance for _____.

I now pray, Father God, that the bond or cord between Your heart and _____'s heart will be a strong, unbreakable love cord, transporting the message that _____ is LOVED, WELCOME and SAFE! May it be engraved on the tablets of _____'s heart.

Thank you that You are involved in every detail of our lives because You love us!

I ask this, Father God, in, and only because of, the Name above all names, Jesus Christ, my Saviour. Amen.

KEY SCRIPTURES	
Psalm 139:13–16	Psalm 127:3
John 6:33, 35, 48, 51	Luke 1:15; 31–33; 37; 40–44

1. Männer, J. 2022. *When does the Human Embryonic Heart Start Beating?* www.ncbi.nlm.nih.gov/pmc/articles/PMC9225347/. doi: 10.3390/jcdd9060187
2. Sandman, C.A. *Mysteries of Foetal Development revealed.* School of Medicine. Louisiana State University.
3. Morris, H.M. 2009. The Genesis Record, p. 86. MI: Baker Books.
4. Van den Berg, G. 2023. *A Change of Heart*, p. 103. 1st edition. South Africa: Suiderkruis Boeke.
5. Di Pietro, J, Sandman, C.S. 2020. *Development of Socio-emotional Regulation: Mysteries of Foetal Development.* American Psychological Association.
6. Lewis, Marilyn, Elsevier, W. 2006. *Relationship of prior custody loss to maternal-foetal bonding in a subsequent pregnancy.* Science Direct.
7. Van den Berg, G. 2023. *A Change of Heart*, Chapter 10. 1st edition. South Africa: Suiderkruis Boeke.
8. *Dr Allan Schore on Attachment Trauma and Effects of Neglect and Abuse on Brain Development.* https://www.psychalive.org/video-dr-allan-schore-attachment-trauma-effects-neglect-abuse-brain-development/.
9. https://www.fredhutch.org

Notes

Phase 4: The Birth

PRIMAL ORIENTATION

Here I am!
This is me.

The cry of the newborn rips through the atmospheric thickness with a frequency of between 400 and 600 hertz (Hz), loudly announcing his arrival. Attention-worthy for the human ear (the average voice frequency is 100 to 120 Hz for males and 200 to 220 Hz for females) He boldly announces, "Here I am! I have arrived!" Phase 4 is the climax and final phase of the *Arrive* part.

Birth is the celebration of a new life and of the incredible life ahead.

> *I will give thanks and praise to You, for I am fearfully and wonderfully made;*
> *wonderful are Your works, and my soul knows it very well.*
>
> – PSALM 139:14, AMP

Show me another creator such as the One who formed the earth, all creatures on the earth and man? There is no one other than Jehovah Elohim, the Great I AM, who loves you with an everlasting love (see Exodus 3:14).

His excitement over your loved one's birth far exceeds your own.

"But even the very hairs of your head are all numbered."

— MATTHEWS 10:30, AMP

We serve a God of detail. Moments matter – especially the moments that form part of the birth process. It matters a great deal in the laying down of vital building blocks for the life ahead. Deep-set imprints are formed during this phase, often only manifesting in Phase 9 onwards.

Profound moments in time usually include a shift from darkness to light, from water to air. From being in hiding to "Here I am, world!"

The Crossing Over

Phase 4 is a passing-over phase from a dark, hidden, unseen space to one that is exposed, visible and filled with opportunities.

The Greek word for "born" is *ghennaho*, which means to procreate, i.e. from the father, but by extension of the mother; to regenerate, to beget; be born, bring forth, conceive, be delivered of, have a gender, make, spring. "Born" in Hebrew is *yalad*, i.e. to beget, to *show lineage*, have a gender.

"Birth" means to carry, to bring, to bring forth, give birth to, to endure without resistance, to support, hold up, sustain, to wear.

The role of the mother is "to bring forth" the child from the hiddenness of her womb to the open light of life. Joyfully. Without resistance.

The role of the father in the sense of "birth" is to father children. This holds much significance as the role of the father is often overlooked or underestimated during the birth of a child. In the Jewish sense, to "father a child" means he brings another *over to his way of life*, to convert someone.

God the Father has made Jesus His Son and God; the Father makes men His sons too, through faith in the redemptive work of Jesus, our Lord! He calls you and your loved one over to His way of life. What a privilege for man to have the invitation to be a son of the Most High God!

You are born and reborn. Your child is born and should be reborn. Every human is destined to have two definite births:

1. The one in the physical – birth without understanding, but choosing earthly life.
2. The next in the spiritual – birth with understanding, choosing eternal life!

Keep the correlation between the physical and spiritual elements in mind as you pray throughout this phase. This final phase of the *Arrive* part carries the cry of your loved one, "Hello! Here I am, I have arrived!"

Symbolically, the visible (physical) manifests the invisible (spiritual). This phase states:

- Life
- Light
- Breath!

As discussed in the previous phase, the little one is expected to choose life from the beginning of his developmental journey. Choices determine direction. Such an enthusiastic positioning supports a positive orientation towards life – for all the primary role-players. This choice will manifest in pushing through and finally arriving at the destination of air and light, and a grateful and loving welcoming committee.

Mother and baby must be perfectly synchronised during the birthing process, from her first contraction to his first breath (10 seconds post-breakthrough). A harmonious agreement between mother and baby during this phase should enable a safe arrival and reveal the fruit of the bonding developed during the previous phase.

Studies have shown how the neuropeptide, oxytocin, plays an enormous role in this synergy and the preparation of the birth process, both in the bonding between mother and newborn and the sufficient nurturing (breastfeeding) that should follow. The presence of effective support during this process is crucial for a synergistic "dance" between the various role-players, but especially the mother and the newborn.[1]

Experiences have the authority to shape our perceptions. They often have a louder voice than the voice of truth or reason. The birth experience is not exempt from this influence and forms a strong part of baseline thinking and interpretations as the young individual develops. His personality adapts eagerly to experience. This is how he will learn what life is all about and who he is in relation to the rest of the world.

The Epigenetic Factor

The birth period holds a strong epigenetic influence. The process strongly contributes to changes in convictions and perceptions regarding self, other, God and life in general. The whole spectrum of experiences during this phase will be long-term determining factors.

Convictions are *your own truth* or reality that determine your view of life. Convictions shape how you approach life and how situations are handled, decisions are made and relationships are enjoyed (or not). Your whole social world is experienced through these deep-set convictions.[2]

Therefore, the birth process can have an enormous impact on your self-definition (the question of the heart). Experiences in this phase help shape the answer to the question, *Who am I in relation to the rest of the world?* This will highly impact primal orientation –

towards thriving or surviving. The theme for this phase is therefore "Primal Orientation".

Arthur Janov's take on how the prenatal phase and the birth process impact life is fascinating. He is a well-known psychologist and psychotherapist, focusing his therapy on the patients' primal pain and how it impacts mental illness. He is still viewed as one of the world's leading clinical psychologists and bases his opinions on more than 20 years of extensive research and the observation of hundreds of patients in his various clinics worldwide. He states, "The younger the age when the trauma is embedded in the person, the deeper the impact on the whole person." This includes the physical: immune strength, parasympathetic versus sympathetic dominance in dealing with life, as well as how stress is processed right throughout life.

Within the Autonomic Nervous System (ANS), the sympathetic and parasympathetic nervous systems balance how you function on a daily basis; knowing when to get things done and be active or vigilant, and knowing when to be cautious or calm. It is this balance that is challenged when you have been exposed to acute or chronic trauma or have a fear-versus-love driven approach to life. Fear as the main motivator in choices will most likely bring an imbalance of either the parasympathetic or the sympathetic nervous system.

If parasympathetic dominance is experienced, the person may battle with low impulse control and therefore may also struggle to focus on one thing at a time, losing concentration by being easily distracted.

Freeze responses as the default response to life's stressors may also be determined by the stress levels experienced during birth. To freeze is the passive response to stressful situations, an inability to react – to fight or to flee. Freeze responses would be typical during a parasympathetic-dominant reaction to stressful stimuli.

> Convictions are *your own truth* or reality that determine your view of life.

Should the Sympathetic Nervous System (SNS) become the dominant baseline in responses, a too high alertness or awareness will be expected. A person with this baseline approach will most likely react first, limiting the role of context and sound reason in the decision-making process.

Janov and his teams have found that a lack of oxygen in the womb and during birth (referred to as hypoxia) can have a long-term impact on how our bodies handle stressful situations. "Having cold feet" can actually be due to the primary distribution of oxygen to the lungs, heart and other vital organs, to the exclusion of the hands and feet. Janov and his teams have seen this phenomenon in many patients whose mothers smoked during pregnancy, causing a lack of oxygen to the foetus and the baby during birth. Low oxygen levels may also be due to the use of painkillers and anaesthetics during the birthing process.[3]

There are sufficient data available to see a strong correlation between the emotional state of the mother and the newborn. Both dopamine and cortisol levels are tested during the birthing period.

These biochemical send-offs are measurable and support the view that deep imprints are left on the spirit and heart of the new individual. If the mother has experienced high stress due to circumstances, it is deposited to the infant – high cortisol can be the chemical result – or if the mother experienced depressive mood states during pregnancy, a low level of dopamine can place the newborn at risk for depression (depending on environmental stressors during his life).

If strong synchronisation exists between the mother and the infant, there seems to be a well-adjusted harmony between the function of the sympathetic and parasympathetic nervous systems, each operating when necessary to ensure healthy functionality. If either of these nervous systems were forced to dominate during the birth process, it may become the default in dealing with life: The mother may be told to "hold back" until the doctor or medical team is on site. The baby is ready to be born, but the rest of his supportive environment are not. In some cases, this may set the parasympathetic as the default, causing the new individual to have a mindset of procrastination, a victim mentality or a sense of helplessness – "No matter how hard I try, my circumstances are against me", or "I have no control over life's circumstances".

This may cause a dysfunctional locus of control, i.e. the understanding of which aspects of life lie within your control and which do not. When you understand what lies within your control, you can take full responsibility for them without blame-shifting or making other excuses, as a victim mentality would do. A person with a dysfunctional locus of control can also show avoidance-driven behaviour. He will make choices based on what negative outcome he wants to avoid: rejection, humiliation, punishment, disappointment, failure or shame. We will discuss this further later.

Harmony or synchronised functionality is required to live from your true and original potential. If both the mother and the newcomer have a dysfunctional locus of control, co-dependency is likely to form. The one will then be waiting for the other to act in certain situations, then blaming the "partner" if things did not work out as planned or expected.

Remember that God's DNA as the redeemed characteristic includes a reigning approach to life (see Phase 2). He has made man to be a victor and not a victim, born to enjoy healthy control over his thoughts, behaviours, choices, and interests.

Pray that your loved one's sense of control will be restored and that a clear understanding of the locus of control will equip him to take charge of his life.

DCC versus ICC[4]

Previously the umbilical cord was cut immediately post-birth, but there are now differing viewpoints between opting for DCC (Delayed Cord Clamping – 5 minutes) and ICC (Immediate Cord Clamping – 20 seconds) after birth.[5]

The benefits of DCC for premature and full-term babies, tested at four months, are:

- Improved iron storage during the first few months (higher ferritin, the protein supporting storage of iron in the blood). In humans it acts as a buffer against iron-deficiency and iron-overload. Iron-deficiency in an infant may affect cognitive, social-emotional, motor and behavioural development.
- Improved transitional circulation (the time/process where the foetus' blood circulation is transformed to adapt to the newborn's phenotype (environmental adapted genotype).
- Significantly lower late onset of sepsis.
- Increased brain myelin, the supporting function vital for the newborn – if dysfunctional, it may contribute to the development of dyslexia and autism, among others.

These myelin-producing cells are sensitive to iron deprivation. Oligodendrocytes (types of neuroglia) are metabolic active cells in the brain. Myelin forms the insulating sheaths around the axons – the part of the neurones sending the messages to other receiving neurones via their dendrites.

The afterbirth is delivered around 20 minutes after the baby has been born.

The First Physical Contact

The physical should manifest the emotional and spiritual in life. The first physical touch should confirm the non-verbal message of the heart, with the mother's heart crying out, "I am so grateful you are born! I love you!" Her touch and the first intimate moment must confirm this.

Skin-on-skin carries vital messages.

Some more benefits of skin-on-skin during this encounter include:

- The mother connects with her little one through smell, voice, words and touch; some of her words will be familiar to him as hearing is active during the last trimester. This will also soothe the newborn.
- Through their skin, they bond and communicate non-verbally through enzymes, hormones and heat-causing stimulation of oxytocin.

- Oxytocin levels increase. Oxytocin is the social hormone that supports effective lactation, bonding, wound healing and empathy in both mother and baby.
- Cortisol levels decrease.
- An increase in milk production for necessary breastfeeding and bonding occurs.
- Protection and comfort after the experience of moving from the safe, known space of the womb to the external world.
- It also radiates the message of gratefulness, love and unconditional acceptance through the electromagnetic emanation from both the mother's and the newborn's hearts.
- It enhances self-regulation in the infant due to ongoing development of healthy attachment.
- It supports healthy brain development.
- It increases a sense of security, which supports healthy trust.

C-section birth or natural birth can also have diverse effects on this bonding time. There is, however, no difference in the HRV (heart rate variation) in the delivery mode. The HRV differs more with the health states of mother or baby, circumstances, term state and support. The HRV is a valued indicator of the neuro-psycho-social state of the mother, which has shown to be a direct influencer on the birth process, as well as the postnatal bonding between newborn and mother. With a C-section, immediate skin-on-skin is often lacking due to anaesthetics.

Research has indicated that although separation between neonate and mother has been the norm in cases of low birthweight or other medical urgencies, it has not shown long-term benefits; the baby survived biologically, but experienced toxic stress and therefore the outcome is similar to Adverse Child Experiences (ACE) in future development. (ACE to be discussed later.) A more healthy and wise balance between the maternal presence and effective medical care should be part of the post-birth support. Skin-on-skin and heart-to-heart bonding are as vital for your loved one's survival as physical health at birth, as well as in the long term.

🔑 A Born Ability to Trust

If any of the abovementioned requirements of a healthy birth process did not occur with your baby, ask the Father's forgiveness for any part you might have played in any perception of rejection or abandonment that your baby might have experienced.

Receive Father God's forgiveness. Forgive where needed and forgive who you need to (yourself, others, medical teams, God). Then pray over these aspects.

If any trauma occurs during this phase, the natural development of trust may be jeopardised. Trauma might include disharmony during birth between mother, baby, medical team, circumstances or the occurrence of harshness, disrespect, miscommunication, verbal or non-verbal messages of rejection regarding appearance (arrival and looks), gender, birth manner, lack of synergy, breathing, APGAR results or responses towards mother after birth. Often a mother may experience trauma during the birthing process, such as bleeding or a negative reaction to the anaesthetics she was given (causing emotional absence), all which may be interpreted as rejection by the little one.

Pray then for trust to be restored in your loved one's life. Trust and wisdom are inseparable. How can you follow Jesus as the Way, the Truth and the Life if you do not trust Him? *Trust turns your heart towards receiving Truth.* It opens your heart to His Presence (see Psalm 9:10; John 14:6).

"Placing our trust in other human beings makes every system develop." Dr Henry Cloud emphasises the importance of trust between an infant and his mother during his primary developmental stages. Humans cannot develop or function effectively without sound trust.

Trust enables safe and effective interconnectedness, a vital prerequisite for high functionality in life. Trust also enables healthy risk taking. If trust is developed during these early stages, it will equip the individual to discern between safe and unsafe others.

The 1 + 1 = 2 Principle

Our Creator God implanted in us an instinctive ability to know when someone or something is not in agreement with what it should be – this is how He intended it to be. We are born with a sense of what is right and what is wrong; we naturally sense when the physical frequency is out of sync. This applies to birth, breathing, nourishment, sensing and connecting.

The new being intuitively knows what is right, an innate ability to know what is supposed to happen versus what is abnormal and holds potential danger. This basic survival skill correlates with all other species.

This principle of survival stretches into his environment and in going forward on his developmental journey, "Who and what are safe, who and what will threaten my survival or my excelling?" As he develops, his ability to have and fearlessly apply this intuition may either be secured or it may unfortunately be damaged.

If your little one experiences what is right and good from this phase onward, he will have a strong ability to discern later on in life if something or someone is not safe. This can be compared to knowing 1 + 1 = 2. You do not teach a child that 1 + 1 does NOT equal 3 or 5. You simply teach him the correct answer and, because there is no doubt, he will recognise the wrong answer quickly because he knows the right answer so well.

This principle will continue to apply as he develops. He should not be easily deceived by treatment that differs from respectful love. It runs like a gentle golden thread that is practised by the infant and primary others from infancy throughout life. The role of trust will continue to be unpacked as you journey on.

Risk and trust are inextricably intertwined. If he loses trust in his primary carer, it can possibly put other relationships at risk and will heighten his risk-taking, with him approaching life with a default setting of scepticism. Almost always, this might limit his inner potential, robbing him of the riches that Father God has planned for him.

Pray, therefore, that a new sense of discernment and wisdom will be secured in his life. A fear-driven approach to life will limit his potential and all the good things that life might hold. A love-motivated approach to life will harmoniously enhance the vast potential that the future offers!

Prayer for Phase 4

Our Creator God, You are a God of detail and more involved in our lives than we can even imagine. You have blessed us with life, love, and breath! Thank you for the precious gift of life.

My Father, I bring every little detail of _____'s birth to you. If imprints were made on his life during his birth that may have left him doubting his value or identity, please re-write those messages. Where he may have felt abandoned or lonely, may Your Holy Spirit minister comfort, security and acceptance. If there have been moments where he did not feel welcome or safe due to my or other's hesitations or other resistances during birth, please minister to _____ and restore him from any harm on physical, emotional, mental and spiritual levels.

Father, please bring _____ to a deeper understanding of how to handle situations in life and to discern between what lies within his control and what does not. Restore his momentum in life and allow a healthy balance between alertness and being able to rest. Please restore him in the way he approaches life's challenges.

My Father God, come through Your Spirit and restore _____'s sense of self, how he views others and You. Come and rewrite any distorted messages written on _____'s heart's tablets due to his experiences in this phase. Bring order from any confusion regarding _____'s identity. Let _____ truly know who he is. If any harm has caused his personality to change in such a way that he is experiencing limited potential, come today, my Father, and restore the spiritual imprint of his calling.

My Creator and Re-Creator God, come and transform _____'s ability to trust – to know who to trust and to develop a strong sense of discernment in relationships.

Today I bring _____ before You. I ask You to declare over his life that the day of his birth is blessed and he is a beautiful gift from You. I declare today over _____'s life that he is welcome, safe and loved!

In Jesus' Name. Amen.

KEY SCRIPTURES	
Psalm 139:14	Matthew 10:30
Exodus 3:14	Psalm 9:10
John 14:6	Proverbs 3:5

1. Walter, M.H., Abele, H., Plappert, C.F. 2021. *The Role of Oxytocin and the Effect of Stress During Childbirth: Neurobiological Basics and Implications for Mother and Child.* www.ncbi.nlm.nih.gov/pmc/articles/PMC8578887/
2. Van den Berg, G. 2023. *A Change of Heart,* p.104 onward including Chapter 11. 1st edition. South Africa: Suiderkruis Boeke.
3. Rank, Janov and Leboyer. 1976. *Primal birth and trauma.* Wiley Online Library: https://onlinelibrary.wiley.com.
4. *Effects of Delayed Cord Clamping on 4-month Ferritin Levels.* The Journal of Pediatrics 1-s2.0-S002234761837753. www.jpeds.com
5. *Delayed cord clamping after birth.* 2020. https://www.acog.org. *Deferred cord clamping, cord milking, and immediate cord clamping at preterm birth.* 2023. https://www.thelancet.com.

✏️ Notes

Receive

Treasured loved one,
open your heart
to receive
what God has prepared
from the ages
through The Son,
your ultimate Gift.

Up to this point, through your prayers of realignment, your baby has received a good and godly inheritance, the gift of life, his birthright, a welcome reception at birth, and has been initiated into trust. He is declared welcome, safe and loved!

He is now positioned to receive whatever Father God has in store for him in the next two parts.

This part consists of Phases 5 to 8 and focuses on what your loved one should receive to equip him for the *Influence* part. This does not mean that he is not able to also influence during these stages, as there will always be an impartation from and to individuals – those who are unborn, newborn or moving rapidly forward on the timeline of development or those in the official stages of influence.

Part 2 covers the phases from the first crossing over (birth) till the next crossing over phase at thirteen years of age.

Remember, a phase is a segment in time where the physical development or age of a person will (or should) be ready to receive distinct environmental stimuli, which is essential for effective development. For growth towards a whole, mature and functional human, the environmental stimuli and the individual should be in a give-and-receive alignment.

At this stage, it is good to be reminded as to why you are on this journey: your heart's desire is to see your loved ones flourish in their original spiritual identities and callings, free of limitations or hijackings caused by traumas and past hurt. On this journey, trust and pray that the Father's light will reveal to you, as a prayer warrior, the various aspects and areas in need of prayer.

Our Heavenly Father's light exposes the secrets of the past in order to encourage and enable His restoration. His light is safe and never shames. Remember Hebrews 4:12–15.

Invite His light to enter your heart and cleanse you from thoughts and intentions not in agreement with His redemptive plan. Then seek His light to enter the past and present of those for which you are on this journey. He saves you from the harm of secrets and covered-up sin. You are safe in His light.

Within a safe environment, the heart allows inpouring from outside influences: from the environment, the community, and from God. During this part of development, safety should be the norm.

Should the newborn experience either Trauma A or B, he will react by either closing up or forming internal laws or vows regarding who is safe and trustworthy and who is not. Potentially, this may harm a healthy self-definition, who others are, who God is and what life in general is all about.

Trauma during this part may distort all four areas of impact and leave the individual confused and extremely vulnerable to deception. A sense of what is normal and right becomes twisted, and the original self is either hidden or locked away. The $1 + 1 = 2$ principle is not established in this interpretation. His heart is misled.

During Part 2, some of what is received will be due to the receptor's choice, and some will be due to whatever crosses his path, a flow of unavoidable events that leave him with little or no choice. It should, however, be the aim of the primary caregivers to supply good and wholesome provision. Through this, trust is built and the necessary can be accepted and enjoyed.

To receive willingly requires sufficient trust in the giver.

Trust is built through faith in our relationships. As you journey through this part, the importance of a relationship built on unconditional love becomes crystal clear and should provide strong key points for prayer.

The development of trust forms an inner compass for your loved one and, together with peace, should be part of the inner counsel, to judge and direct.

Phase 5:
0–3 years

TRUST

A strong start can help build a more equal society.
– DEEDEE YATES

This is the phase of discovering and experiencing the world, learning where one as a new human is in the circles of primary others and his immediate world, but with limited movement abilities and interpretations.

Discovering himself and the environment from outside the womb are some of the joys of this phase. It secures the foundation that your loved one's life will be built upon. Phase 5 strengthens the basics of right and wrong, good and bad, safe and not safe, the 1 + 1 = 2 of life.

Continue to keep in mind the core question, the question of the heart, *"Who am I?"* During this phase, the search to find the answer continues, especially in relation to the rest of the world.

A few important role-players in this young human's life includes his primary caregivers, other family members and family friends, as well as the immediate environment. The young child is also acutely aware of the spiritual environment.

Physical contact is finally possible, and the delight of connection increases dramatically. Similar to the previous phases, man's physical development should mirror our Creator God's investment, love and joy over you and your loved one.

This phase expects a steep climb in physical, emotional, mental and spiritual growth, a climb that includes many challenges. The role of the primary caregivers will also face enormous challenges. It is therefore crucial to grasp the responsibilities of those appointed to care and nurture the most vulnerable.

Physical Development

The brain develops bottom up, with the basic survival areas developing first.

The seat of emotions, the limbic system, follows: first the basal ganglia and hypothalamus, then the amygdala into the second year. These regions also play a huge role in judging what threatens the child's survival. Trust is continually tested and developed according to experiences. What or who is safe or not? "Trust" as a basis for intuitive bonding is the theme of Phase 5.

The limbic system develops the most during this part of the twelve phases. It is the part of the brain shaped in response to environmental experience by also adding emotional weight to an experience. The rational analysis of a situation or environmental stimuli and choosing the ideal emotional weight requires a healthy synergy between the senses, various brain regions, the intuitive ability of the heart and the spirit.

The environment strongly influences our physical development.

A safe environment ⟶ stronger trust ⟶ healthy brain biology and development.

Bruce Perry, an American psychiatrist, working at the Child Trauma Academy in Houston, said, "The brain is formed in a use-dependent manner." Man develops according to the stimulation received from his environment – good or bad. If responses or reactions are demanded, the brain is activated, and connections and neurone pathways are formed.[1]

Within your social environment, your loved one bonds with emotions. The vital attachments formed during this phase become the safety net for healthy risk-taking and exploration. Trust enables these secure attachments.

Predictability reinforces trust because it strengthens a sense of control, which again strengthens security. Positive routines reinforce trustworthiness, healthy growth and bonding.

Trust also enables the young child to receive all he needs to be equipped for a well-functioning life. This is the age where he is positioned to receive sufficiently. To receive requires the provider and the receiver to be in sync. Such a partnership should enjoy one another's company. What the provider shares must be receive-worthy.

If a young person in this phase senses that his caregiver(s) cannot be trusted, he instinctively knows that he is not safe and therefore in danger – physically and mentally. He may close himself off to receive the bit of good that is available, and forms his own definition of the world and himself.

Dendrites and Bonding

Your loved one is highly sensitive for environmental stimuli. He enters this world with about 86 billion neurones, with some of these neurones not yet connected and eagerly awaiting stimulation.

Much research has focused on the first 1 000 days of life (from conception to 24 months). This phase, however, includes the third year (starting from after birth), and is viewed as the most sensitive regarding brain architecture: maths, social skills, language, concept formation, response, habit development, emotional management, sight and hearing orientation (which is the highest between one and two years of age).

The plasticity of the neurones is also the highest during the first 1 000 days. The young developing brain uses about 97% of the little one's energy in relation to 44% of that of a four-year-old. It is a critical time to receive sufficient care and stimulation.

The Economy of Good Parenting

The well-known Namibian education and development consultant, DeeDee Yates, says it so well, "A strong start can help build a more equal society." To be part of establishing a strong society is why you are on this prayer journey.[2]

Man never grows or suffers alone – every human is knowingly or unknowingly interconnected and both influence and are influenced by the world around him. This is inevitable, and a huge requirement for effective development.

"We are wired to connect," Daniel Goleman stated. Man's need to survive stretches far beyond mere food and physical safety. Survival, especially mentally and emotionally, depends on his social environment and the connections therein.[3]

Professor James Heckman, a professor in the economy of human potential, refers to this phase of development as follows, "The global economy benefits from effective early parenting!" It deserves your highest attention.[4]

During this phase, the parents or caregivers have very specific responsibilities. Dr Allan Schore (also mentioned in Phase 3) states that the interactions between the primary caregiver and the baby play a crucial role in the development of the social brain.

The social brain is a network of physical areas that enable us to recognise others and evaluate their mental states, feelings and actions. Remember the role of oxytocin in enabling empathy and bonding? It is good to mention at this point that not only the brain is involved in "reading", tuning into and connecting with others; there are also other aspects of self-participating. Effective social bonding requires more than just the brain's involvement.

The emotional and relational environment of a young person (the first three years) form an environment-dependent brain. It supports a strong functioning vagus nerve and immune system. Emotional congruency should also strengthen as the social brain develops.

Dr Allan Schore's 2012 model of psycho-pathogeneses makes it very clear that the study of interpersonal neurobiology confirms that early social-emotional experiences influence later experience – by altering the developing brain.[5]

> Through an effort of independence, a person moves from dependency to eventual interdependence.

Schore says, "The emotional relational environment provided by the primary caregiver shapes, for better or for worse, the experience-dependent maturation of the brain systems involved in attachment functions that are accessed throughout the life span." [6]

A child develops within a relational environment, depending on most of his skills to mature through healthy and effective relationships. This is similar to our primary purpose – to develop into mature Christians, influencing the world to reconcile with Father God through Jesus. Each individual needs to enjoy an intimate relationship with our Heavenly Father.

Through an effort of independence, a person moves from dependency to eventual interdependence.

Dependence ⟶ *Independence* ⟶ Interdependence

Throughout the phases, there is a constant exchange between the developing human and his environment. This exchange already began in the previous phases, but during Phase 5, physical touch and eye contact (light) can enhance the connectedness. May such an exchange help to create an environment filled with the Father's lovingkindness – breathing in and breathing out.

Basic Need Containers

You are born with little empty "containers", your basic need containers.[7] It is your primary caregivers' responsibility to pour into these little containers, out of their own.

These containers contain the following, to mention but a few:

1. Unconditional acceptance.
2. Acknowledgement for the small and big achievements.
3. Knowing you are here for a reason, that you have purpose. Your life matters. YOU matter.
4. Respect from and for others and self; the language of love. (The five love languages versus the five disrespect languages will be discussed in the next phase.)
5. Security on provisional, spiritual, physical and emotional levels. Security = survival.
6. To belong, to be included and orientated towards a trustworthy environment.
7. To know who you are, your true worth and your original identity.

I Am Loved, I Am Welcome, I Am Safe

Unconditional parental love causes inpouring into the young one's need containers. "Unconditional" includes no fluctuation in the sense of being loved and acceptable, whether being needy or demanding or being content. This also includes whether it is testing boundaries or being submissive.

Sufficient filling up will support healthy "serve and return" – I receive and then I give (this will be discussed in Part 3).

Love as a *noun* includes a feeling of tenderness, passion, warmth and respectful caring.

Love as a *verb* includes to care about and want to support, care for, comfort, spend time with, connect with, get to know more, protect and serve. Love for another person will include actions of expression, words (verbal) of affirmation and respect within verbal and emotional (non-verbal) communications.

A solid foundation of this kind of love is necessary for effective bonding and eventual discipline and mentoring.

The 1 + 1 = 2 principle also applies here. If a child experiences honest, respectful and unconditional love as he is growing up, he will effortlessly recognise when behaviour is unacceptable. Something will seem "off".

If a child does not receive the "real" need in his need cup, he might attempt to fill those little containers with alternatives, such as performance, rebellion, anger, defiance or having a sceptical approach in relationships, to name a few examples.

Bessel van der Kolk, a psychiatrist and expert on traumatic stress, says, "Children who don't feel safe in infancy have trouble regulating their moods and emotional responses as they grow older, show more psychological stress in HRV (Heart Rate Variation) and stress hormone responses." [8]

We will discuss this and Adverse Childhood Experiences (ACE) in the following phases.

Joy Camp

During this phase, the young child has to learn to return to joy from any negative emotion experienced. When he slips and falls, he needs his mother's comfort to return to joy. A mother will help this along spontaneously when she diverts his attention from pain and humiliation to joy.

When this happens regularly, the young one will learn to move from feeling angry, afraid, jealous, ashamed or humiliated, to joy. Joy becomes his default return – the resting place. Dr James Friesen has called this "developing joy camp". [9] Pathways are built to return to joy camp – the way in which emotional resilience is developed, and being able to return from experiences such as disappointments and failures.

When this normal comfort does not occur in times of need, the toddler will attempt his own alternative "resting" places: bitterness or self-pity, rage or hopelessness and despair. This will not support healthy self-regulation.

Behavioural Mirrors

When a parent respectfully attends to the needs of her loved one, even before it is requested, the parent's intuitive behaviour reflects a true image of the child's worth. Such a mirror is level.

I call the mirror referred to here a "behavioural mirror". As an example, a baby cries for whatever reason, and the mother enters the room. If she enters the room with a gentle willingness to attend to her baby's need, her behaviour will be respectful. If, however, she is irritated or agitated and impatient to get the crying over, her behaviour will be disrespectful. Both carry non-verbal messages that imprint onto the little one's heart as to whether he is worthy to be respected or not. A child looks at the mother's behaviour and views that as a reflection of his own worth. This forms a huge part of his self-definition, *Am I attention worthy? Am I to be respected as a person with needs?*

Disrespectful behaviour ⟶ distorted self-image

A distorted sense of self can be due to a curved mirror with a distorted reflection.[10]

With these aspects in mind, what do you pray for concerning this phase?

🔑 Suggestion for Prayer

A guideline to prayer is provided here instead of a specific prayer. Apply these keys to guide your personal prayer for you loved one(s), as you call their names before our King and continue to build a prayer altar concerning this generation, as well as the following generations.

PRAYER POINTS

1. *Pray for healthy trust to be restored in your loved one's life as a guide to discern and secure healthy bonds. Pray that this restored trust will draw your loved one to the only One who can always be fully trusted. Pray and declare Proverbs 3:3; 5, 21–23; 26 over your loved one.*

   Trust Father God that the filling up of the real basic needs as your loved one entered life will be restored according to how He created you, i.e. unconditional love, respect, purpose, acknowledgement, and security. Trust that your little one will feel celebrated!

Psalm 23:5, AMP: You prepare a table before me in the presence of my enemies. You have anointed and refreshed my head with oil; My cup overflows.

Filling up happens when spending time in His Presence. Pray that your loved one will have a strong desire for His Presence.

Psalm 103:1, 5, AMPC: Bless (affectionately, gratefully praise) the Lord, O my soul; and all that is [deepest] within me, bless His holy name! . . . Who satisfies your mouth [your necessity and desire at your personal age and situation] with good so that your youth, renewed, is like the eagle's [strong, overcoming, soaring]!

Psalm 81:10, AMP: "I am the LORD your God, Who brought you up from the land of Egypt. Open your mouth wide and I will fill it."

2. Trust that he will know he is loved and worthy of respectful attention, and that this will be part of his restored self-definition.

   Pray that the Truth written on his heart's tablets about his worth will be Luke 1:28, MSG: "Good morning! You're beautiful with God's beauty, beautiful inside and out! God be with you."

3. *Pray that your loved one's joy camp will be restored or maybe created for the first time. That new pathways will be formed from any negative emotion back to joy. That joy will be his default mood state (joy is not necessarily happiness, but may include the emotion of being happy). Pray also that the harmful alternative "camps" will be removed in His time, according to His timing and your loved one's capacity. First a joy camp should be built, then the harmful ones must be removed.*

   Isaiah 61:1, 3, AMPC: . . . The Spirit of the Lord God is upon me . . . To grant [consolation and joy] to those who mourn in Zion. In Luke 4:18–20, we see that Jesus read from Isaiah 61:1 and 2. He then stated that the prophesy is fulfilled through Him. Part of that prophecy and what Jesus came to restore was to provide His everlasting oil of JOY (read the rest of Isaiah 61).

John 15:11, AMP: I have told you these things so that My joy and delight may be in you, and that your joy may be made full and complete and overflowing.

Romans 15:13, AMPC: May the God of your hope so fill you with all joy and peace in believing [through the experience of your faith] that by the power of the Holy Spirit you may abound and be overflowing (bubbling over) with hope.

Galatians 5:22, AMPC: But the fruit of the [Holy] Spirit [the work which His presence within accomplishes] is love, joy (gladness), peace . . .

4. *Pray that your loved one will bring praises to our King with understanding and a healthy awe. Pray that Father God will build a stronghold around him for protection and the cultivation of a God-orientated lifestyle, singing songs to Him with childlike faith.*

Psalm 8:1–2, TPT: Yahweh, our Sovereign God, your glory streams from the heavens above, filling the earth with the majesty of your name! People everywhere see your splendor. You have built a stronghold by the songs of children. Strength rises up with the chorus of infants. This kind of praise has power to shut Satan's mouth. Childlike worship will silence the madness of those who oppose you.

1. Perry, B., D. *Maltreatment and the Developing Brain*. Grand Valley State University. https://www.gvsu.edu. Physical Connections between Neurons.
2. Yates, D. *Do the first 1,000 days determine your future?* https://youtu.be/XCscN4zuvd4
3. Goleman, D. 2006. *Social Intelligence*. London: Hutchinson.
4. Heckman, J. 2012. *Invest in Early Childhood Development*. The Heckman Equation https://heckmanequation.org
5. Dr Allan Schore. https://www.allanschore.com/
6. Dr Shore, A. 2012. *Models of Psychopathogeneses*. "Essentially, interpersonal neurobiology explains how early social-emotional experience indelibly influences later experience - by impacting and altering the developing brain. The emotional relational environment provided by the experience-dependent maturation of the brain systems involved inn attachment functions that are accessed throughout the lifespan. https://www.allanschore.com/
   https://www.psychalive.org/video - dr-allan-schore-attachment-trauma-effects-neglect-abuse-brain-development/
7. Van den Berg, G. 2023. *A Change of Heart*, p. 54, Chapter 5. 1st edition. South Africa: Suiderkruis Boeke.
8. Van der Kolk, B. 2015. *The Body Keeps the Score: Mind, Brain and Body in the Transformation of Trauma*. USA: Penguin Random House.
9. Friesen, J., Wilder G., James E., Bierling, A.M., Koepcke, R., Poole, M. 1999. *The Life Model: Living from the Heart Jesus Gave You*. Shepherd's House. Dr James Friesen is a Psychologist from Southern California. He is also an author of several Christian books on healing from severe childhood trauma, including DID (Dissociative Identity Disorder).
10. Van den Berg, G. 2023. *A Change of Heart*, pp. 54–56. 1st edition. South Africa: Suiderkruis Boeke.

✏️ Notes

Phase 6:
3–6 years

RESPECT

Curiosity
Come ask the question: Why?
and you will see
doors swinging open
bringing light and delight
Ask no questions...
and you might just miss
as Opportunity glides away
towards the others asking: Why?

'The important thing is not to stop questioning. Curiosity has its own reason for existing. One cannot help but be in awe when one contemplates the mysteries of eternity, of life, of the marvellous structure of reality. It is enough if one tries to comprehend only a little of this mystery every day.'
– EINSTEIN[1]

"Ask and keep on asking and it will be given to you; seek and keep on seeking and you will find . . ."
– MATTHEW 7:7, AMP

Seeking is the prerequisite to finding.

If your loved one is indeed curious and searching for answers to his natural mind and heart's questions, what does the area look like where he may seek?

Opportunities provide the space for childlike inquisitiveness.

 Secure Investigation

Phase 6 brings many growth and developmental opportunities for your loved one. He should be encouraged to ask, seek, discover and grow. If he is provided with a safe platform to ask and wonder, he will be positioned to receive what is needed and happily equipped for his future.

The ultimate goal for your children is for them and the following generations to know, *"Who am I?",* by knowing who He is. This is the heart cry of every human being.

Phase 6 builds boldly upon the previous phases. Each phase is a building block towards enjoying the fullness of life that Father God prepared for you and your loved ones. His aim is to prepare you to spend eternity with your God and Saviour!

One of the golden threads running through the developmental phases, glueing the various building blocks together, is trust. Trust plays a determining role in developing healthy social bonds and skills. Trust enables receptivity – a person who feels safe will receive. When you feel safe, healthy risks will be taken to enjoy exploring the world around you.

During this phase, a child further discovers life and where he fits in. Remember the question remains, *Who am I in relation to the world around me?* – mommy, daddy, family, others, life's demands and God.

The exploration of life expands during this phase, especially regarding his self-definition. He learns to receive and also to give. The send-and-receive interaction between child and caregiver is vital for the development of ultimate interdependency later on in life. A person goes through dependence, puts in an enormous effort to be independent, but should eventually enjoy a life of interdependency.

During this phase, the child also discovers certain characteristics and abilities about himself: he can climb higher or run faster than his friends; he keeps rhythm well or that when he sings, others cheer. Every experience is relative to his physical and social environment.

Trust is the precondition for, and creates space to, respect the uniqueness of himself and others.

The main theme for Phase 6 is "Respect".

Respect includes:

- showing regard for those who are "different".
- regarding your own birthright and those of other.

- regarding that which is your own as well as another's personal "locus of control", the control zone, that which are his responsibilities, and under his control. There are various controllables that should develop and mature around eighteen years of age (more about this in Phase 9).

This regard for himself should develop and become more settled and secured. It is a journey of discovering where he begins and where he ends, what is part of him and what is not, not only physically, but also emotionally, mentally and spiritually. The journey enjoys momentum during this phase.

The Language of Respect and Disrespect

How do we communicate respect? Respect is to respond, not react, with a patient demeanour.
Remember these five points:

- Eye contact when engaging and connecting
- How you touch
- Words used in conversations, giving tasks or disciplining
- Tone of voice – very important – gentle, patient and clear
- Time – to listen, to engage, to ensure he feels that he matters

Respect further supports the ability to treasure – to regard or to value will manifest in the act of treasuring and to respectfully care.

The opposite is to neglect the cues from the preschooler. Regular and intentional send and return is required for the meeting of basic needs. If this to-and-fro rhythm is disrupted or absent, a child will experience disregard – a form of trauma. Neglect impacts the new developer on a dangerous level regarding brain development and social abilities (remember trauma types A and B).

According to Jack Shonkoff (American Paediatrician, professor at the Child Health and Development at Harvard, *From Neurones to Neighbourhoods: The Science of Early Childhood Development*), neglecting a child's basic needs will not only fail to provide the vital stimulation required for strong brain architecture, but it will also fail to provide the child with one of the most important activators of healthy biology for stress management.[2]

Shonkoff and his team shared four types of unresponsive care on the spectrum of neglect:

1. *Occasional inattention:* normal, even good; a child also learns to self-soothe and explore his environment; keeps himself occupied.

2. *Chronic under-stimulation:* children have less interaction with adults/significant others than required for healthy development. They will/can hopefully catch-up in time in a stimulating "serve-and-return" environment.

3. *Severe neglect in a family context:* long periods of inattention and lack of responsiveness by significant others.

4. *Severe neglect in a constitutional setting:* mass accommodation of children/children's homes.

Shonkoff stated, "Neglecting young children is neglecting the foundation of a healthy next generation." [3]

Various articles discuss how attachments between the child and the primary caregiver first develop during pre-birth between the right brain and the other person's right brain, and continue through the phases of development. Also, according to the National Library of Medicine, emotional experiences are contained in the right brain and bond through emotions with the other person's right brain. Humans also bond heart to heart. More about this later.

Caring correctly demands the understanding that the young one's needs are more important than the mother's (within context and reasonableness), and it must show.

Reactions such as, "I don't like it if you cry like that" or "Stop nagging me, everyone is looking at us" will diminish how the young one communicates his needs, making the issue more about the mother's needs or insecurities than her child's.

A child must be able to count on the mother and/or father for nurturing, comfort and healthy attention. Being attuned to others will build trust and support empathy. These are the building blocks of a strong society.

Brain Development

Your loved one's brain has almost grown 90% by the age of five. He uses a huge amount of glucose to support this rapid growth demand (twice as much as that of an adult).

Listening skills and vocabulary enjoy a high-speed increase, growing from managing 55 words at 16 months to 225 words at 23 months and 573 words at 30 months.[4]

The following shows the age and number of words recognised through conversations and verbal communications:

- Age 1: 50 words
- Age 3: 1 000 words
- Age 5: 10 000 words[5]

It is crucial to have appropriate conversations with him during this phase – to progressively allow interactions that will ignite the "Why's".

If this phase in conversing and searching was stunted, your loved one may have formed his own assumptions about his self-definition, who God is, or what the world and others are like. Assumptions are mostly misleading and attempt to fill the gaps of unanswered questions that may lead to distorted viewpoints. If such an environment becomes the norm, it might silence the voice of curiosity and leave the individual extremely vulnerable as he filters life through a blocked filter of rejection, disregard or abuse.

He desperately needs a safe space to investigate what life is all about.

Goals for Phase 6

Emotional and social milestones and parental roles in Phase 6:

- Copying friends and adults: Mirror neurones play an enormous part in learning
- Showing love and affection and care towards others (empathy develops into action)
- Grasping concepts of yours and mine; the basis for boundaries in relationships
- Showing a range of emotions: sadness, happiness, anger, jealousy, frustration, fear and increasingly being able to name and communicate this to his primary others
- An inquiring approach towards self, others, environment, things of interest, life and faith
- Fulfilling small tasks: eventually up to three at a time

Mirror neurones in the cortex support the role of empathy in social bonding. The hormone oxytocin further supports the development of empathy, as well as reading others' facial expressions and choosing the appropriate response. Growing from three to six years of age, the child will learn the *intention* behind the behaviour. Based on previous experience, his mirror neurones will be activated (firing) when he recognises intention and behaviour. This is necessary for building solid relationships.

During this phase, the child's ability to monitor his surroundings as safe or challenging is one of the priorities for a healthy development of trust.

Van der Kolk (mentioned in Phase 5) states, "Children who don't feel safe in infancy, have trouble regulating their moods and emotional responses as they grow older." They may struggle with high levels of cortisol, leading to anxiety and a dysfunctional HPA-axis.

The HPA-axis is activated when alarm signals are discerned. When the acquired response to potential danger is completed and a sense of safety is restored, the axis needs to come to rest. A constant stimulation of this axis can result in over-stimulation. An anxious and high alert approach to life may become the default way of living (the baseline thinking of dealing with life). Lower HRV (Heart Rate Variation) may also result – weakening the overall immune system and emotional regulation.

A child needs to have a sense of inner safety regarding his own ability to manage his emotions, sensory data, and how he responds to his surroundings. This will provide a safe development of confidence and an increased locus of control. An inner sense of control will strengthen an outer influence.

> A child is not an extension of the parent(s). Respect for where he begins and where he ends is necessary.

As stated previously, the brain is shaped by experiences. It is also largely shaped by relationships. Phase 6 presents the preschooler with opportunities to strengthen his emotional and social brain. Being able to identify and describe his emotions gain momentum during this phase.

It is an ideal time to increase the child's emotional vocabulary by playing games such as looking at faces and describing their possible mood states. This will strengthen emotional congruency (congruency means coinciding or working in harmony for the best impact).

During this age, the preschooler can start by doing small tasks handed to him. A significant response to his efforts or the completion thereof should be part of the ritual. It will provide a sense of satisfaction and the encouragement will grow.

The parent, being the most present life mirror, should constantly reassure the young one that he is welcome and is a blessing to have as part of the household.

Words such as, "I am so glad you were born", "I enjoy spending time/being/playing with you", "I love you", "I like you" and "What a blessing/joy you are!" are important words.

These affirmations for just being present or being born imprints self-regard and self-acceptance on the child's heart. It builds further on the foundation of unconditional love and acceptance, constantly securing the normal, the $1 + 1 = 2$.

Again, this will pave the way for a healthy relationship with Father God – understanding that His love is also, like the parent's, genuine, safe and unconditional.

Another milestone of Phase 6 is the development of the difference between fantasy and reality. Most children in this phase enjoy active imaginations. With this also comes an ability to see and detect spiritual things, such as having visions or seeing angels.

So many of these spiritual gifts are lost due to scared or sceptical parents who scoff at the stories that are eagerly shared.

Pray that these precious spiritual gifts, as part of our loved ones spiritual identities and callings, will be restored. With this, pray for the restoration of their creative abilities – to step out and celebrate their creative abilities. Also pray for godly discernment regarding any vision or imagination, to develop sharp spiritual intellect guided by pure love for Father God and His Word.

This is the season to secure the foundation of a basic faith and the hearing of the Word. From the story of creation to the salvation through Jesus should be the child's primary sense of purpose, belonging and security. Rhythms of talking about and with Jesus, Father God and the Holy Spirit should be established with plenty of room for the "why's?" and other inquisitiveness.

The parent should encourage regular conversations after watching something together or hearing something being said. Room for differences in views or opinions will encourage independent thinking and engaging with other's opinions.

This is the phase of releasing and developing the inquisitive mind; "Why?" is the golden question for discovery and growth. "Why?" should always be welcome as part of discussions. It unlocks the quest for truth and activates a strong scaffolding between the prefrontal lobes and the limbic system. More about this in the following phases.

A child is not an extension of the parent(s). Respect for where he begins and where he ends is necessary, first regarding the physical aspects, then mentally and spiritually. This forms a vital foundation for a healthy locus of control – taking responsibility for the aspects within his control without blame-shifting or being domineered by another. The latter may lead to shame or a sense of helplessness.

A sound locus of control will also strengthen the preschooler's sense of safety and security, an essential part of building self-confidence, and enjoying healthy trust in himself and others.

The Heart as Communicator

Man consists of a physical aspect and a spiritual aspect, linking man with both the physical and the spiritual worlds. Each aspect of man reveals the primary focus and responsibility of that aspect:

- *The body:* How will this situation affect my safety?
- *The spirit:* How will this situation affect my faith?
- *The emotions, thoughts and will (often referred to as the soul):* How will this situation affect my relationships?
- *The heart:* How will this situation affect my self-definition? Who am I (in relation to this situation)?

Knowing who you are will launch your full potential. "To be fully you, you have to stay alive (the body's task), benefit from relationships with others and self (task of the heart), and live in unity with God (task of the spirit)." [6]

Knowing who you are will provide a healthy, selective admission of other's and the world's opinion of you. Mirroring your self-image continuously in the level life mirror of Jesus' eyes will restore every distorted image the past has shown.

"A malfunction in our collective being threatens our earthly existence and impacts eternity."[7]

There is a synchronisation between individual HRV; if there is skin-to-skin, there is a brain-to-heart impact. If there is space between the individuals, the heart-to-brain connection impacts via the intertwining electromagnetic fields. The physical heart is the most intuitive organ in the body, manifesting your spiritual heart. It carries an electromagnetic field in a parameter of 0,934 metres, fully impacting the direct environment. You pick up others' fields and influence the atmospheres around you.

The heart is the core of your being.

A person assesses while observing his environment and those in it. He will focus on that which grabs his attention. When something or someone enjoys high regard, focused attention will spontaneously be given (for example, by role models).

> Respect determines focus (being love motivated).
> Focus determines imitation.
> Repetitive imitation establishes habits, lifestyle and default behaviour.

Unconditional love and respectful behaviour are the level life mirror, teaching your loved ones to regard themselves and others.

The Word as Your Mirror

The Word of God is the most level of all life mirrors. Repetitive imitation of the Word according to the main message of redemption through Jesus our Saviour is worthy of imitation! You need its reflection on your inner man – on your activated mirror neurones and on the tablets of your hearts!

This loudly declares that you regard His Truth and Who He is. It also declares who you are in Him, determining what the heart pursues. You have been assured how valuable Father God regards you by the exchanging of your life with the Blood of the Lamb of God. The Blood of Jesus was the ransom price paid for you. You matter to Him! (see 1 Corinthians 7:23; 1 Corinthians 6:20).

You and your loved one need to continuously look into His Word: to see and to imitate, to eventually become you (and your loved one's) default choice of behaviour, until it infiltrates the very core of your identity (see James 1:23–25).

Regard for Father God's Word is key; it determines your focus. Regard it with your physical eyes and ears, as well with your heart's eyes and ears (see Matthew 13:15).

Pray that your loved one's eyes will have a baseline focus on His truth. Pray that every distorted image portrayed during this stage will align with the Father's love for your loved one so that their hearts can heal and be whole again. Wholeheartedly pray Deuteronomy 30:6 over your children. This is the primary aim.

Prayer for Phase 6

Father God, You are our Covenant-keeping God, the only true living God.

Thank you for allowing us to know You and to serve You as our King and Saviour.

Today, I bring _____ before You, Father. He is precious to You and I pray that he will experience the abundant life You have given as a gift. I ask for Your guidance and wisdom to be with _____, so he may discern Your will and for Your spiritual gifts upon his life to restored.

Please heal and restore _____ from any damage due to neglect or disregard during this development.

Father God, please guide _____ into a lifestyle of respect: for You, for others, for himself and for the beautiful gift of life. Help him to know who he is by growing in revelation of who You are.

Guide him by Your Holy Spirit to love and respect Your precious Word. Let _____ 's heart trust the Truth of Your Word as the level mirror, to be worthy of imitation.

In Jesus' Name, Amen.

KEY SCRIPTURES	
Matthew 7:7	Matthew 13:15
Deuteronomy 30:6	James 1:23–25
1 Corinthians 7:23	1 Corinthians 6:20

1. 2019. https://www.weforum.org.*10 of Albert Einstein's best quotes*. The World Economic Forum.
2. Sconkoff, J. 2000. *From Neurons to Neighborhoods: The Science of Early Childhood Development*. National Research Council. Institute of Medicine. 2000. Washington DC: National Academy Press.
3. Centre on the Developing Child, Harvard University. *https//developingchild.harvard.edu*
4. Prof Goswani, U. https://www.cne.psychol.cam.ac.uk. Centre for Neuroscience in Education. https://theirworld.org. Accessed February 2017.
5. Shipley & McAfee. 2015. *Vocabulary size and auditory word recognition in preschool children*. https://www.ncbi.nlm.gov. Accessed May 2016.
6. Van den Berg, G. 2023. *A Change of Heart*, p. 130. 1st edition. South Africa: Suiderkruis Boeke.
7. Van den Berg, G. 2023. *A Change of Heart*, p. 137. 1st edition. South Africa: Suiderkruis Boeke.

Notes

Phase 7:
6–12 years

SYNCHRONISED
VALUES AND TRUTH

My world is small.
Yet vast, because I dream and "like" and "follow"
Enter my world and you will know
There is always space for more of you
and less of those.

Each phase builds upon the other. Just as man never operates in isolation, no phase stands on its own.

The main themes of the phases so far:

1. Phase 1: Preparation
2. Phase 2: Redeemed DNA
3. Phase 3: Bonding
4. Phase 4: Primal Orientation
5. Phase 5: Trust
6. Phase 6: Respect

What does Phase 7 hold for your loved one?

A New Level of Vulnerability for Influence

Your loved one has been prepared for life, positioned to receive love, to secure safe bonds (trust) and to value life (respect), as well as to honour the Giver of life!

Phase 7 pertains to the process of synchronising values and truth. The theme for Phase 7 is therefore "Synchronised values and truth".

Truth plays a huge role in developing wisdom, the central theme of Phase 8. Truth and the Word of God are inseparable, the Word being the primary source of truth.

This is the season where discernment increases between fantasy and reality (mentioned in Phase 6), without losing the inner visualisation, the gift of imagination.

Building on Phase 6, "Why?" continues to play a crucial role – to have the freedom to ask this regularly and for the parent to stimulate questions and encourage the development of an inquisitive mind. To explore the vastness of life and all it contains should be fun and something the child enjoys taking part in and often initiates.

Asking "Why?" ignites conversation, connection and an ability to discover his own mind. The understanding develops that these different approaches to one subject is not only normal, but also good. Taking other's opinions into consideration becomes part of context – a key to understanding and consideration. This is again part of the golden thread of trust and respect.

The well-known French writer and poet from the 1760s, Voltaire, stated, "Judge a man by his questions, not by his arguments."

Daniel Goleman's statement, "Assume nothing, question everything", is one of my favourite sayings. Assumptions often lack context, leaving us poor in making wise decisions.[1]

The child should be encouraged to frequently ask "Why?", often also being asked that question by the parent. Kurt Gödel (also called Herr Warum), a well-known Austrian Logician from the 1930s, said a parent should regularly ask the child, "What matters in life, in his life, others, etc. and why does it matter?"[2]

Regular positive experiences of this kind of conversation will stimulate out-of-the-box thinking and solution-orientation towards challenges. It also stimulates healthy development of context-orientated decision-making, a vital aspect of brain development during the following phases.

The Role of Family Dynamics

This is the season where family dynamics plays a huge role in the formation of the child's identity.

Who am I in relation to this small circle of community?

There are significant differences seen in the birth order of siblings: firstborn versus middle child versus third born/youngest – in confidence, spontaneity, sense of responsibility and dedication (versus procrastination). This may be due to changes in parenting styles (which we will look at a little later), lifestyles and activities, time management of household, and culture.

It seems that the firstborn usually takes the role of the most responsible of the siblings, with the middle ones trying to follow and fit in on both sides, but often struggling to receive the same amount of attention from their parents. The youngest sibling seems to enjoy a much more relaxed parenting style and will therefore either have less self-discipline than the others or a more laid-back approach to the pressures of life. Keep this in mind as you pray through the sibling effect on your loved one and how it might have impacted his sense of self.

This is the last phase of dependence; from the following phases onward, the pendulum will start swinging towards the opposite side – independence (an eager effort during Phase 9), and will eventually settle in the middle – interdependence. This should be the norm, but will not always be the case.

Further notes on the role of family dynamics: In a family of four (two parents and two siblings), there will be sixteen dyads. The more dyads in a family, the higher the potential conflict. According to Jeff Kluger (American author of *The Sibling Effect*), a type of argument often occurs every 6,3 minutes.

He also stated, "Siblings are the people you road tested life before travelling further on your own." So true.[3]

> When the parent treats all children equally, sibling rivalry dramatically diminishes.

The largest trigger for arguments seems to be over property, for example, toys or play space. Through these experiences, respect and emotional property concepts are learned. Boundaries regarding what should be one child's responsibility and what should not are also learned through these experiences.

The second trigger is issues with justice. Man is encoded for justice. When he experiences injustice, the regions activated are those dealing with disgust, and he processes experiences of shock and trauma.

This is true regarding unjust handling of punishment (it so often occurs with the eldest/ firstborn children getting the blame for things they did not initiate or are not responsible for). And so, justice and ownership enjoy vigorous development during this phase.

Also enjoying active development during this phase is the relationship between parent and child. Children worldwide seek parental attention. Positive and respectful attention are of course first, but even negative attention seems to be better than no attention at all.

In the book, *Hold on to Your Kids,* authors Gordon Neufeld and Gabor Maté urge parents to execute intentional relationships with their children right from the start until they leave earth.[4] Parent-child relations are pivotal in their vulnerable years in stabilising identity and in choosing relationships outside the core family group.

According to studies, almost 95% of parents have a favourite child. How this is portrayed or handled in the family dynamics is where harm or trauma can be done. When the parent treats all children equally, sibling rivalry dramatically diminishes.

Prayer during this phase can also be for our loved ones to feel unconditionally accepted and loved. No favouritism between parent and child should ever be displayed or felt by any child – whether the favourite at heart or not. Instead, unconditional love should be communicated verbally and in non-verbal ways.

Parenting styles should teach a child the 1 + 1 = 2 principle of love. To love is an active way of living that strengthens security, honesty and closeness. Love bonds people in an empowering manner and will always encourage the child to be his original self and grow to his full potential.

Two Ways to Bond

Humans can have one of two types of bonds with others. To illustrate this, two rivers flowing parallel can be compared to two ways of dealing with relationships, opportunities and life in general:

1. The Love River flows gently onward, with rapids here and easy flows there, all gently moving towards the destination of excellence. You enter this river already qualified as good enough, loved and valued. There is no need to perform or convince. Your pace can be quiet, sitting on a rock and enjoying the open skies or with eager momentum, enthusiastically on your way.
2. The Fear River flows with a set goal, to avoid rejection, punishment, disappointment, failure or humiliation and shame. The one swimming relentlessly in this river is mostly motivated to avoid such "bad" outcomes. The destination: perfection (a destination impossible to reach).

A normal and acceptable ratio between the rivers (fear:love) should be 1:5.

It is unavoidable to never spend time in the fear river, and a parent's guidance should include how to deal and utilise failure, disappointments and rejection – these are part of life and can be golden building blocks in strengthening character and a secure identity.

If ratios are out of sync, you should get out of the Fear River, run across the ground and jump into the Love River, until being in the Love River is your default setting.

Pray that your loved one will be capable of handling the unavoidable failures, disappointments and rejections of life without carrying shame or other limiting emotional outflows.

What role does a parent play in the development of a child during this phase? Various parenting styles can be identified and there are multiple books available on this subject. However, for the purposes of this prayer journey, I have decided to share five styles of parenting based on my therapy experiences. These are by no means founded on executive research nor as peer-reviewed data. They are mentioned only for the purpose of understanding that different parenting styles will have various influences on development.

Five Parenting Styles

THE FOUR LIMITING STYLES

1. The Lid
- The dominating, controlling parent – "I know better/best . . ."
- If your child's ideas, plans and dreams do not correspond to yours, the answer or response will be negative and domineering.

2. The Drone
- The overbearing, overprotective parent – "I am scared/afraid that . . . might happen to my children . . . they might get involved in . . ."
- What ifs; you can never be sure . . .; Maybe . . .
- A lack of trust in yourself as a parent, in the child and/or in God.

3. The Open Gate
- The uninvolved parent.
- "Sorry, I can't be there, I am just too busy . . ./really busy with this incredible . . ."
- "Children are not a priority . . ."; "They must learn how 'real life' works . . ."
- "I work so hard to provide for *you*. Stop demanding and be grateful for what you have/can enjoy!"
- Regular guilt-spoiling with unnecessary gifts or privileges.

4. The Magnet
- The unstable parent (needy due to mental or emotional instability, dependence (alcohol, drugs), physically ill, physically/mentally disabled).
- "What about me?"
- "You must be grateful for all I have done for you . . . Don't leave me alone, don't go away."
- "You owe me."
- "What did I do wrong for you to want to leave me?"
- "I need you!"

- Co-dependency manifests in this type of parenting. The parent is demanding and manipulating by using guilt to get attention and/or feel needed. They may (mostly subconsciously) not motivate a healthy letting go or following their own unique interests that might hinder closeness or dependency.
- "I feel so hurt when you talk about studying away from home."
- "It makes me sad/left out when you rather want to go and play at your friend's house."

These four parenting styles limit a child's growth potential. It may bear the fruit of bitterness, rebellion, anger or a co-dependent next generation. Limitations in emotional management and incongruency may become part of their adult life, causing poverty in friendships and also in the eventual choice of a life partner.

Along with parenting styles are other societal influences that also play major roles in shaping your loved one during this phase:

- School system (academic, sport and culture): huge pressure on performance (Fear River's destination)
- Sport systems: as above
- Social environment: pressure to fit in and belong

Achievement = Latin word = *consecutio* = the process and the result or outcome = receive the intended (receive what was pursued) = reaching the goal.

This is normally a team effort and does not require only one individual.

Other —————————— CHILD —————————— Other

A huge amount of influence and participation occurs OUTSIDE the child's locus of control (control zone).

A question worth asking here is, *How reasonable or fair is it to praise/acknowledge/ honour one child (without the rest of the team)* or, *How fair it is to measure the success of something that requires a whole team or group of participants (with awareness or not)?*

Achievements should be acknowledged according to what lies within your control, such as attitude, diligence, determination, discipline, commitment, control of behaviour, and time, more than the outcome (points on the field or marks on the school report).

To focus on and praise what lies outside the control zone may increase anxiety. Disappointment may result in depression due to a sense of helplessness, and it could strengthen a sense of conditional self/other acceptance and love, building a distorted identity ("If only I can . . .").

Rather rejoice and celebrate the fruit of hard work, diligence and commitment, a good attitude and fortitude. This will strengthen and encourage the locus of control, as well as love-motivated choices.

Further supporting factors towards a distorted social system and environment are:

- Value distortion – determined by society and culture
- Traumas A and B – dysfunctional HPA-axis/hyper- or hypoactive (dangerous)
- Experiences of disappointment and failure, causing a false measurement of worth

These become the "fuel" in your life's fear-driven "vehicle". This vehicle is definitely not on its way to celebrate and support the development of your potential! It also may not provide space for growth.

As Virginia M. Axline, one of my favourite authors and mentors on child therapy, said, "Not all movement is forward." You need to make sure you (and your child) are in a vehicle taking both of you forward.

The author of *The 5 Love Languages*, Gary Chapman, taught the global community how to love wisely according to each individual's uniqueness. His wisdom has saved a multitude of relationships, including those between parent and child. I am extremely grateful that he shared his years of expertise with us.

Love communicates verbally and non-verbally, "You matter".

The following, however, is the opposite of these love languages. They are the languages of disrespect. Love and respect are inseparable. So are disrespect and rejection. Both of the latter may be unintentional, but will scar the receiver.

Disrespect communicates verbally and non-verbally, "You don't matter".

Please approach these five disrespectful languages without a judging heart – towards yourself or others. This is only a tool to invite your Re-Creator into the scarring and to have the joy of witnessing His work as He restores and renews.

The Five Disrespectful Languages

A person communicates with disrespect when:

1. Divided attention: The person being talked to is preoccupied, for example, the parent is on the phone, social media, laptop, working, watching sport/television, or just disengaged; the person's mind is elsewhere. A child may say, "You are *not* listening". Remember, to listen is to respect. "Did you hear what I said?" There is no response when asked an opinion or a response on a discussion or question.
2. Touch only when protecting or disciplining, i.e. no regular hugs, kisses or cuddles.
3. Communication without eye contact or mainly communicating when giving a task.

A parent will mainly make contact or converse when a task is given or when arrangements have to be made. There is an absence of normal, daily and comfortable conversations.

4. Any manner of humiliating the child — shaming, breaking down, belittling, exposing his weakness privately in an authoritative way or in public before his friends. Treating a child's rational need irritably or with impatience.

5. Attention, help or support with an agenda.

The Impact of Disrespect

In such cases where a child's growing-up years are in love- and respect-deprived homes, the long-term impact can be far worse than you may realise. Adverse Child Experiences (ACE) may include all four harmful parenting styles mentioned previously. The fruit may linger long into adulthood and may influence your life quality, choices and even faith.

A study published in the *American Journal of Preventative Medicine* in 1998 provided data of 17,500 adults regarding their ACE scores. Their subjects' ACE scores were registered and their history of physical, emotional and sexual abuse were collected for this study, called "The Adverse Childhood Experience Study". Both types of traumas played a significant role in this study, although, as mentioned before, Trauma A, the absence of what was needed (i.e. neglect of basic needs), showed a shocking impact.[5]

During this study, Drs Vincent Felitti and Bob Anda correlated the ACE scores with general life quality, such as health, career functionality, mental stability and overall social interdependencies. Results revealed the crucial role the home environment and a safe parenting style plays in the long term: high ACE scores (> 4; indicating high presence of traumas A & B during childhood) = a higher probability of suffering long-term illnesses such as diabetics, heart problems, sleep problems, depression, certain cancers, lower emotional resilience and lung illnesses.

The occurrence of ACEs is unfortunately very common in society; the study was done in 1998 and with a limited grouping of a people groups and culture, but it is still good to take note: 67% of the population showed results of at least 1; 12,6% showed results of 4 and more.

The strong correlation between ACE scores of higher than 4 shows a relative risk of:

- Chronic obstructive pulmonary diseases (2,5% higher than ACE of 0)
- Hepatitis (2,5% higher)
- Depression (4,5% higher)
- Suicidality (12% higher)
- Lung cancer (3% higher with ACE score of 7 or higher)
- Ischemic heart disease (3,5% higher)

ACE has also been studied in regard to the brain development of infants. The most well-known impact of high ACE scores has shown inhibition in the normal development of the prefrontal cortex – vital for higher thinking processes such as interpretation, reasoning and impulse control. The area in the brain necessary for pleasure and reward processes are also affected – this shows the strong correlation with substance abuse in later years.

A summary of a study done in Australia, 2024, showed that, *"Up to 40% of prevalent mental health conditions, including anxiety, depression and substance abuse, stem from childhood maltreatment. The study estimates that addressing childhood maltreatment could prevent over 1,8 million cases of these disorders. Specifically, childhood maltreatment accounts for 41% of suicide attempts and 35% of self-harm cases nationally. This comprehensive analysis underscores the urgent need to treat childhood abuse and neglect as a public health priority, with potential policy interventions to alleviate family stress and support mental health."*[6]

Trauma in all its forms harms the ability of the individual to deal effectively and naturally with the challenges of life. Trauma causes dysregulation stress responses and thus affects the healthy functioning of the HPA-axis, as mentioned previously. According to Peter A. Levine and Anne Frederick, the authors of *Waking the Tiger*, trauma memories are contained in the right hemisphere, where bonding operates.

The right hemisphere's suppression of trauma is strongly connected to the body, which may be the reason why the body's suffering can indicate the suppression of trauma. It may also impact healthy bonding needed to enjoy your life partner in marriage. A distorted sense of self may bring the need for alternative personas in an effort to belong, as you may feel ashamed of who you are – you are not good enough. (More about this in Phases 8, 9 and 10.)

A Redeemed Version

But praise God that He is our Re-Creator and nothing, no memory or past incident is higher in rank than the Name of His Son, Jesus Christ. This prayer journey calls on His recreative power and aligns you and your loved one's past story to His Story (see Ecclesiastes 3:11; Isaiah 61:4).

Your story will still be the same, but it will be a redeemed version through the Blood of the Lamb of God.

Please take time to repent of these behaviours during your parenthood season. Accept the Father's forgiveness because of the complete work of Jesus. Forgive any wrongdoers who sinned against you during your growing-up years and may have encouraged or challenged you during your parenting season. Forgive yourself as well.

True repentance restores authority. Repent with a sincere heart and a convicted spirit, be truthful and willing to admit and confront. Open your heart to the Father's exposing light and enjoy the privilege of His forgiveness and unmerited favour. Oh, how He loves you, precious intercessor (see Psalm 51:10; Acts 3:19; 1 John 1:9).

Prayer of a repenting parent:

My Father, You are always the same – yesterday, today and forever. Thank you that You are my anchor and my compass; You light the way forward, but You also shine Your light into my past and into my heart. Thank you that Your light is always safe and never shames.

As a parent, I have not taken up my full responsibility. I have caused hurt and pain to the children/child (_____) you have entrusted to me, Father. There were times where I was ignorant, tired, busy, agitated or just lazy and did not meet _____'s basic needs in that season. I am sorry, my Lord, for neglecting Your treasured one(s).

If applicable: There were times Father, where I deliberately damaged _____ by emotionally hurting him, unfairly accused and punished, rejected, ignored and neglected him when he did not perform well enough, or disappointed me. There were times that I publicly humiliated and shamed him. I ask for Your forgiveness, my Father.

If applicable: There were times, Father, that I as a parent did not value and respect _____; not as Your loved one, a gift from You or as pure.

I confess before You these sins I have committed. Please forgive me.

Father God, You are the Covenant-keeping God of Abraham, Isaac and Jacob. Thank you for restoring the godly covenant between me and You, my marriage and our children.

Forgive me as the parent of _____ for not aligning my children _____ as I should have and for being careless in my walk and responsibility. I ask forgiveness, my Father, that I did not display the level mirror of unconditional love and acceptance towards _____ and so may have misguided _____ regarding who You are.

Thank you, my Father, that through Your Son, Jesus, my Redeemer, I may be forgiven for my sins and washed clean! Thank you for the Blood of Jesus that was the complete and acceptable offer for all my sins!

I now ask that you heal _____ in every area where these sins have caused harm to his body, spirit, emotions, mind and heart. Open _____'s eyes to see You – to recognise You as the one and only true God.

Open _____'s ears to hear and recognise Your voice, Father God.

Even if _____ has not hungered for You, let _____ meet You, see You and hear You. May _____ taste and see that You are good! And may _____ hunger for more of You.

Father, please restore the inner compass of _____'s heart to discern truth from lies and to know where to go.

Let _____ enjoy Your presence and may he treasure Your Word as _____'s life necessity!

In the Name above all names, Jesus Christ, my Saviour, Your son! Amen.

Now move on – with a clean heart and renewed authority.

Moving on effectively should include praying for restoration in your loved one's life, if they experienced you displaying one of the first four parenting styles and experienced the disrespect in certain times and seasons of being a child under your care.

5. The Fifth Parenting Style: The Outstretched Hand

A healthy parent has a healthy self-regard, self-definition and unconditional self-love (according to Matthew 22:39). To love yourself is a command.

At the funeral of the well-known evangelist, Billy Graham, his son honoured his legacy in a profound manner. Franklin Graham described the character of Graham with three words, stating that his father always was:

- Available
- Dependable
- Approachable

For me, the author, this defines an ideal parent – an ADA parent:

- Having a likeness to Father God.
- Teaching the truth; the 1 + 1 = 2 principle of imitation-worthy behaviour.
- Mostly holding a level mirror towards their child in their behaviour.
- A healthy parent says, "I am here" but also knows when and how far to let go.

An approachable parent will encourage healthy and stimulating conversations, sometimes in a comfortable kitchen setting. A child will feel emotionally safe to discuss and share what is going on in his life, with his friends and in the classroom. Such conversations will create space for imparting insight and guidance. A safe space to share your heart opens the young one's heart to learn how to deal with life's challenges. This will cause an easy flow of exchange between parent and child — learning from one another and growing as humans together.

> *For a child to be open to being parented by an adult,*
> *he must be actively attached to that adult.*
> — DR GORDON NEUFELD AND GABOR MATÉ, *HOLD ON TO YOUR KIDS*

When a child, or any person in fact, senses a safe and comfortable atmosphere, the table is set for "Why?" questions and conversations. This manner of parenting will also stimulate top-down connections (from higher brain to lower brain regions), from the prefrontal lobes to the limbic system, incorporating appropriate emotional weight due to an understanding based on context and perspective.

Dan Siegel, Clinical Psychologist at UCLA and expert on mindful awareness, said, "Name it, tame it." [7] The parent needs to scaffold what a child might feel or experience and soothe appropriately. Scaffolding parenting provides structure, support and encouragement, and builds a bridge between your child's existing knowledge and skills and new knowledge and skills. A child's responses will develop into more rational and appropriate ones when strong and sufficient long-term top-down connections have formed. ("Top-down" is the term used to describe the brain's processing priority, to be reached later in development, and will be discussed in the following phases.)

This type of parenting, in turn, will strengthen love bonds, and trust — "My parent is safe (trustworthy, dependable and approachable); I can ask their advice on this or that matter."

Remember Phase 6: Building emotional vocabulary to strengthen emotional resilience and congruency. This is the name-it-tame-it scaffolding mentioned here.

Healthy parenting will display love towards a child in all five love languages (see Gary Chapman's book, *The 5 Love Languages*).[8]

Healthy parenting will celebrate and acknowledge a child's accomplishments that lie within his control. Marks on a school report card does NOT lie within his control. What does lie within his control is diligent hard work, an attitude of determination and self-discipline.

When regular, appropriate praise is given to her child, a parent is filling the tank of her child's life vehicle, heading towards a fulfilling life. Even the bumps or potholes of disappointment and failures on the road ahead will not take him off-road. He will be mobilised to add his unique value and enjoy being who the Father created him to be.

Pray Deuteronomy 28's blessings and let the Word of God be his 1 + 1 = 2 in Truth. The Love River will be his default river.

Prayer for Phase 7

Our Glorious Father, You are the King of kings and the LORD of lords, the Almighty God, our Redeemer.

We have the greatest privilege to come before You only because of the Blood of the Lamb of God, Jesus Christ, our Saviour!

Thank you that I can bring my loved before You regarding this time of development.

Father, please forgive me where I have not been an available, dependable and approachable (ADA) parent to my loved one(s), where I have not always provided a safe space to explore and learn and discover, especially regarding Your Word and who he is in You.

Please restore my loved one's ability to trust and to respect wisely, to know when he is safe. Help me, precious Holy Spirit, to be an ADA parent to my children.

Where distortion of his identity occurred during this phase, please align his identity with who You originally created him to be, through Your recreative power.

My Father, guide _____ out of the Fear River and reveal to him the availability of the Love River. Train him through Your Holy Spirit's teaching to become so familiar with the Love River that he will quickly be uncomfortable whenever he finds himself in the Fear River. Imprint on his heart tablets, my Father God, that he is qualified to enter and live life from love. He is valued and love-worthy because of who You are.

Please unlock my loved one's inquisitive, hungry mind and heart – to search for the truth until he fully finds You, Truth itself. (You say in Your Word: if I seek You, I will find You.)

Where needed, Father, bring reconciliation between parent and child, sibling and sibling. Turn the heart of the fathers to the heart of the children and the children's hearts to the fathers. Restore godly unity in families, Father, as the godly building blocks of society.

Let my loved one know You, the ultimate ADA Father!

In Jesus' Name, Amen.

KEY SCRIPTURES	
Psalm 51:10	Acts 3:19
1 John 1:9	Matthew 22:39
Ecclesiastes 3:11	Isaiah 61:4
Deuteronomy 30:6	Deuteronomy 28:1–14

1. Goleman, D. 2006. *Social Intelligence*. London: Hutchinson.
2. National Science and Technology. 1974. https://nationalmedals.org
3. Kluger, J. 2012. *The Sibling Effect: What the Bonds Among Brothers and Sisters Reveal About Us*. Riverhead Books, U.S.
4. Neufeld, G., Maté, G. 2019. *Hold on to Your Kids: Why Parents Need to Matter More Than Peers*. Vermilion.
5. Felitti, V.J., Anda, R.F., Nordenberg, D., Williamson, D.F., Spritz A.M., Edwards, V., Koss, M.P., Marks, J.S. 1998. *Relationship of Childhood Abuse and Household Dysfunction to Many of the Leading Causes of Death in Adults. The Adverse Childhood Experiences (ACE)*. American Journal of Preventative Medicine.
6. 40 Percent of Mental Illnesses Linked to Childhood Maltreatment. 2024. https://neurosciencenews.com/?s=mental+ill-nesses+linked+to+childhood. University of Sydney.
7. *'Being' versus 'Doing' with your child.* https://youtu.be/PGUEDtGSwW4.
8. Chapman, G.D. 2015. *The 5 Love Languages*. Chicago: Moody Publishing.

Notes

Phase 8:
12–13 years old

WISDOM

From sons to heirs
From his to His
From shadow to light
From under to alongside
Welcome to Wisdom's delight.

"For whoever finds me (Wisdom) finds life and obtains favor and grace from the LORD.

– PROVERBS 8:35, AMP

The *Receive* part is the last of the four phases and the highlight of Part 2. It should celebrate what is to be received — not only so far, but also in what lies ahead, a celebration of the uniqueness of the individual and his role in the Kingdom of God.

During this crucial phase, the individual needs to receive the key that will unlock whatever his Creator and Father God has prepared for his future. A key symbolises the activation of something previously unavailable.

The key and the lock must be in agreement. Synchronisation occurs when the creator of both intends effective unlocking. During this phase, the key, the lock and the unlocking will all be discussed.

For your loved one to move into a future that holds tremendous potential, he needs to:

- Recognise the right from the wrong key, as many counterfeit keys and counterfeit locks will be set before him.
- Know and trust the one who hands over the key: to guide, mentor and protect.
- Accept and receive only the right key.
- Understand the responsibility of owning this key and what the unlocking will present.
- Unlock and journey with the required preparation.

To unlock requires a stepping through or a crossing over into the newly unlocked space, moving from one position into another.

Stepping Over

This is another crossing over or stepping-over phase. The first crossing overtook place during Phase 4.

Stepping or crossing over includes entering a new dimension and a repositioning. The Oxford Dictionary definition of *dimension* is "a measurable extent of a particular kind, such as length, breadth, or height; an aspect or feature of a situation".

In this context, a dimension is a measured part of the depth between one aspect of life and another, between a state of childhood and a state of entering adulthood.

Birth is a stepping over from water and a hidden, dark state, to air and a visible, light state.

Stepping over includes movement and, in both cases, the movement is forward, towards a new and exciting future.

This phase's stepping over also includes entering into a season of adulthood, which means taking responsibility according to a deeper understanding of your locus of control, exploring your broader social environment and the new, exciting opportunities that now await.

Your loved one is moving to a new spiritual state that we will discuss as you move through this phase.

This stepping over includes agreements. Your loved one will say, "I am ready to enter into what lies ahead. I understand who I am in relation to the challenges." This is an agreement, first and foremost, with Life Himself, with Father God, with oneself and his environment. A holy agreement between one person and God is a covenant.

To step over will include change and a repositioning. Pray that the change taking place here will take your loved one forward, closer to Him who ultimately prepares you for eternity.

The Key

Each previous phase was in preparation for this phase's stepping over and stepping into.

During this last phase of the *Receive* part, the person will receive an invisible and spiritual key to unlock a gate to a new dimension and the opportunities that go with it.

To take full advantage of this new spiritual environment and its opportunities, certain milestones should have been reached. These requirements prepare the individual to recognise this godly key, to grasp the responsibilities that unlocking requires, and to know how to keep going forward into the uncertain and often daunting future.

Milestone 1

This milestone represents a sense of self that is founded on unconditional love, acceptance and regard.

It is not an overindulgent focus on self. A healthy self-regard will encourage sufficient space to grow according to life's opportunities and an intentional effort to invest in the discovered strengths and to manage the identified weaknesses.

If you enter this phase with a distorted sense of self, a healthy focus on other's needs will be a challenge. An emotionally wounded person battles to love and care wisely. They may either have co-dependent relationships or take offence easily due to a victim mentality.

In order to develop a true sense of self, your loved one must know who he is, his strengths and weaknesses, his interests and irritations . . . reaching a place of unconditional acceptance and celebrating his uniqueness. This will buffer the intense social demand lying ahead.

> ### Pillar of Identity
> Knowing who you are and enjoying a sound sense of self-regard, securing your birthright as a foundation, can be compared to a pillar with a fine, porous exterior. Opinions or behaviours outside the pillar will be filtered by the very selective exterior, either allowing the outside to enter and impact or influence the inner definition of self, or keeping it safely outside.

A healthy self-regard will also consider values, gender-identity, truth, dreams and gifts. What you must "look" like, act like or do will be aligned with the surefooted view of who He created you to be. That definition is secured and rooted in the level mirror of His Word and what the message of redemption revealed.

Milestone 2

The second milestone is to increasingly view and evaluate situations in an abstract manner instead of in a concrete way.

To support this, the limbic system matures rapidly from here on. The scaffolding between the limbic system and frontal lobes increases and secures the formation of strong connections, and supports the following:

- To grow in understanding and apply logic to situations.
- To approach life with an awareness that choices have consequences – there is a cause and effect to life. By now, this should have been taught well through fair and respectful discipline and engaged parenting.[1]
- To know that justice is not always a single-sided interpretation; it often requires multiple angles of interpretation.
- To enjoy progressively more appropriate emotional weight attached to experiences.

Milestone 3

Your loved one should be able to know how to accurately apply his locus of control: what he has control over and what are or are not his responsibilities.

Metaphorically, he has his very own property, with a fence and a gate around it. What the garden, house and interior look like are your loved one's prerogative alone.

During this phase, the key to his very own gate is handed over. It becomes his to open up to whoever he wants to permit into his own space.

Everything within this space is fully under his control and is his responsibility. This will include time management, friendship choices and how he handles relationships, conflict and communication, how he chooses to behave, and how he manages emotional experiences and responses. This also includes his attitude towards life, what he believes and how he invests in his faith and relationship, and also how he views himself, others and God.

His property should have an appropriate gatekeeper, known as peace. Any alternative gatekeeper will allow influencers to enter and disrupt the harmony and functionality of the property. Jesus is the Prince of Peace. From this phase onwards, it is your loved one's full responsibility to manage his gate of Peace.

> *Peace I leave with you; My [own] peace I now give and bequeath to you. Not as the world gives do I give to you. Do not let your hearts be troubled, neither let them be afraid. [Stop allowing yourselves to be agitated and disturbed; and do not permit yourselves to be fearful and intimidated and cowardly and unsettled.]*
> *– JOHN 14:27, AMPC*

Jesus' communication to His Disciples is a sure indication that you have a choice in either keeping His peace (once you received Him in your heart), or losing His peace by allowing the world's cares or other negative influences to enter your "property" and disregard Peace as your Gatekeeper. His property, area of control and responsibility is maintained in his heart – the centre of his identity. Knowing who he is in the light of who Jesus is as the Prince of Peace will ensure a secured position of the ultimate guardian.

It will be the responsibility of your loved one to ensure that Peace guards the gates of his heart.

The beautiful golden *key* to open and close his gate is received during this phase. How profound is the responsibility!

Milestone 4

In this milestone, your loved one meets Wisdom as his primary companion on life's journey.

> *Making your ear attentive to skilful and godly Wisdom and inclining and directing your heart and mind to understanding [applying all your powers to the quest for it]; yes, if you cry out for insight and raise your voice for understanding, if you seek [Wisdom] as for silver and search for skilful and godly Wisdom as for hidden treasures, then you will understand the reverent and worshipful fear of the Lord and find the knowledge of [our omniscient] God.*
>
> – PROVERBS 2:2–5, AMPC

Seeking and pursuing Wisdom in your most inner heart will guide and protect and will delight Father God.[2] (Also read Job 32–38.)

🔑 Wisdom Comes from the Breath of the Spirit of the Almighty God

Wisdom includes insight, understanding, the right application of knowledge, discernment and discretion. All of these should be pursued and desired. "Wisdom" is the theme of Phase 8.

Living life with Wisdom as your companion will guide you in your choices in friendships, relationships, participation in various faith-based opportunities, career choices and general life options. But most of all, knowing Wisdom will keep eternal life in your very being – enabling you to be His light in a very dark world.

In short, your loved one should be fully aware of his main priorities regarding faith and how this will manifest in how he lives; time management (Bible study and prayer – pursuing the Truth, building relationship with Wisdom Himself), in relationships with others (value in friendships, gender identity, sexual purity), dedication to his calling, dreams, goals and interests, and living with the values he understands and has made his own.

Jesus' love is tattooed on his heart tablet, impacting his heartbeat so that his life is attuned to that rhythm. Priorities are set by the values he was taught in the previous seven phases.

Receiving the Key

How does your loved one receive the spiritual key to open the new dimension?

The new young adult will be receiving the key to unlocking the future with an understanding of what his responsibilities are. Note that this is also the phase where spiritual calling will be activated. A godly spiritual calling includes:

- The spiritual "fingerprint" that allows the individual to flourish in his uniqueness
- Inflow from the spiritual realm – Spirit to spirit – to enjoy continual provision of spiritual guidance, ability and energy and, most importantly, to get to know Him!
- The source of influence to the heart; then from the heart to the rest of the individual and his environment, in this way changing the atmosphere!
- Blessing those around him with guidance, wisdom and hope; building the Kingdom
- Strengthening joy and fulfilment in your loved one

It can go the opposite way, as the enemy will always attempt to hijack what the Father originally designed. There have been multiple cases where spiritual hijacking has occurred and brought confusion, torment and devastating harm to an individual. His immediate environment (including his family) was also injured due to the ungodly spiritual inflow and activation of the enemy's calling on the person. This can only be due to a lack of knowledge and understanding or a determined evil heritage plan (see Phases 1 and 2). All can be reversed so that the person's godly calling can be reactivated – only by the grace and love of our Creator and Father God.

As a parent, you must be vigilant in pursuing your child's true godly calling. Pray, therefore, for the unfolding of your loved one's calling. This will bring joy and satisfaction to him in being part of the building of the Kingdom of God, for His glory!

This is the phase where your loved one must embrace and celebrate his true identity – aligned with who Creator God intended. Accepting this requires him to have sufficient knowledge of both the strong and weak aspects of his personality, interests and tendencies. It includes his gender identity and how he relates to life, the environment, the social world, others, himself and God. The vital question of the heart, *"Who am I?"*, should largely be answered by now. This is the golden key that will unlock his true potential. The more secure he is in this knowledge, as well as in unconditional love and acceptance without confusion or self-rejection, the more effortless the unlocking will be.

A New Direct Covering

In Phase 8, the young adult begins to move out from under his parent's cover, where he was positioned with spiritual covering. Until now, his parents had taken full responsibility for him and were being held solely responsible by God for their child.

This phase will challenge the parent as much as the young adult. To let go requires trust and confidence in the child's willingness and ability to take on responsibilities, but mostly it requires trust in Father God.

This moving over is gradual. In this phase, the dimension changes –from dependence to eventual interdependence, with a good stretch of attempting independence.

Because of the seriousness of this process, a ceremony is included in both Jewish and Christian traditions. The planning, preparation, cost and time demanded by this ceremony will burn the message of the experience onto your loved one's heart: *I am a valued young adult, with responsibilities and a divine purpose, surrounded by caring mentors. My life matters!*

Such a ceremony includes guests who are and have been invested in the young adult, and who are dedicated to praying for him and to keeping him accountable in a respectful manner. There is some form of relationship between the guest(s) and the person receiving the spiritual key.

It is a call to step over from the accountable covering of his mother and the father. Understanding this daunting reality, the son (or daughter) will declare his faith and dependence on God and his new responsibilities as a new adult. Before stepping over, he will make a public statement of his faith, values and morals. The "stepping over" can be done as a prophetic act by stepping over a rope or ribbon to adults waiting across the line and calling him over.

The young adult will give verbal permission to the witnesses present to pray for him and keep him accountable within the boundaries of his family structure, an investment through time, building relationship, prayer support and mentorship.

This is also one of the godliest opportunities for a father to publicly bless his child and to declare in a loud voice, "This is my son/daughter, who I am very proud of/pleased about!"

KEY SCRIPTURES	
Matthew 3:17	Luke 3:22
2 Peter 1:1–6	

For all three of our children, this was one of the most precious moments of their early days.

I so often hear my clients (young and old) saying how they would have loved their fathers to speak those very words to them. It is a cry of every human heart to make your father proud – you were created with an even deeper cry to please your Father God. Now in Jesus, you have been fully equipped to do exactly that. Praise Father God for that!

In preparation for this phase, during Phase 7 a great deal of time should have been spent discussing relevant matters concerning adulthood. Remember the safe space to ask many "Why's"? A parent working with this phase's requirements in mind should initiate time and discussion points that will equip the child for handling the golden key of adulthood wisely.

Craig Hill's book, *Bar Barakah: A Parent's Guide to a Christian Bar Mitzvah*, explains the importance of this ceremony.[3]

In the Hebrew tradition, this ceremony is called *Bar Mitzvah* – son of the Law – or *Bat Mitzvah* – daughter of the Law. When the revelation of Jesus becomes part of the principles of this ceremony, the name is changed to *Bar Baraka*, son of the Blessing and *Bat Baraka*, daughter of the Blessing.

It is the blessing of the father and the teaching and prayers of the mother that equip the child to enter adulthood successfully, aligned with His calling (see Proverbs 2).

Prayer for Phase 8

Regularly pray and bless your loved one with 2 Peter 1:2–4:

Father God, may grace and peace – which is perfect well-being, all necessary good, all spiritual prosperity, and freedom from fears and agitating passions and moral conflicts – be multiplied to _____ in full, personal, precise and correct knowledge of You, Father, and of Jesus, my Lord.

Your divine power has bestowed upon _____ all things that are requisite and suited to life and godliness, through the full personal knowledge of Your own glory and excellence and virtue.

Through this, Father, You have bestowed on _____ Your precious and exceedingly great promises, so that through them _____ may escape, by flight, from the moral decay (rottenness and corruption) that is in the world because of covetousness (lust and greed), and that _____ will become a sharer (partaker) of the divine nature.

My Father God, I ask You today that You command Your strength and might in Your service onto _____, so that he is impenetrable to temptation.

I ask You, my King, that _____'s golden key to true maturity will be restored to him, and that he will grasp the responsibility of moving onward towards adulthood.

My Lord and King, _____'s father did not have this understanding when _____ stepped over into adulthood. Therefore, I now ask You to bring this blessing over him today, for You are the ultimate Father of all fathers and the only perfect Father. Please walk with _____ to bring him to a place where You can truthfully declare over _____, "This is My son/daughter in whom I am well pleased!" Thank you for creating _____ and that You breathed Your Breath of Life into him.

Thank you that Your Holy Spirit will work in _____ to establish him in the full sense of "sending off" as the mother was supposed to do during this phase. May he experience a sense of stepping over and finding joy in becoming a value-adding, Kingdom-building adult.

(If you as a mother or father have not fulfilled this responsibility, ask forgiveness and pray for restoration. Please note that it is not about the ceremony, but about the principles that are part of it.)

Father God, I ask You today that _____'s pillar of identity will be re-erected and secured on the foundation of his birthright. I ask that he will be restored to who You as his Creator originally created him to be and that he will know who he is in knowing Who You are.

Father, redeem in Jesus' Name _____'s spiritual identity and his gifts and calling with which You created him. May every effort or successful removal by the enemy of this be fully restored.

I pray that he will have a firsthand revelation of the profound love manifested in the complete redemptive work of Jesus, my Saviour. And that Your Holy Spirit will guide him in all Truth. Truth provides the substance of wisdom.

I pray to You today, my precious Father, that Wisdom will be _____ 's companion on this stepping over journey, and onward. May _____ never be willing to exchange wisdom with frivolous talk and senseless living (see Proverbs 2).

According to Job 32, I pray that the Breath of the Spirit of the Almighty God will be breathed into _____ for wisdom. No matter what age _____ may be now, I pray this into his life today.

I ask You, Father God, that _____ will continue to grow and live with the full package of wisdom, having insight and understanding, sensitive discernment and discretion. May _____ know where to go, having a divine compass with You as his main focus.

My Father God, I pray for _____'s heart that You require as a prerequisite for the blessings of Deuteronomy 28; may _____ seek You with his whole heart! I now declare every blessing over _____.

Today, Father, I bless _____ with the Priestly Blessing as it is written in Numbers 6:24–26:

The Lord bless you and watch, guard and keep you, _____.

The Lord make His face shine upon and enlighten you, _____, and be gracious (kind, merciful, and giving favour) to you, _____.

The Lord lift up His (approving) countenance upon you and give you, _____, peace (tranquillity of heart and life continually).

Today, Lord, I call in every blessing and prayers of intercession for _____ from previous generations, grandparents, parents, preachers, prophets and other godly ones in _____'s life, to be restored over his life. I pray that these seeds of prayers be quickly activated and manifested in God-honouring fruit in this new generation.

May he fear You, Father God, with a healthy awe and desire to please You in all he does, and that these blessings will follow. May _____ taste and see that God is good!

In Jesus' glorious Name, the Name above all names. Amen.

KEY SCRIPTURES	
Hebrews 13:5	2 Samuel 7:14
Psalm 2:7	Proverbs 1:7
Proverbs 2	Proverbs 8 and 9
Psalm 102:28	2 Peter 1:6–7; 2–4
Matthew 3:17	Luke 3:22
John 14:27	Job 32–38
Psalm 103:1–6 (especially verse 5)	

1. Dr Jen Trachtenberg, Paediatrician and parenting expert from New York.
2. Van den Berg, G. 2023. *A Change of Heart*, Chapter 12. 1st edition. South Africa: Suiderkruis Boeke.
3. Hill, C. 1998. *Bar Barakah: A Parent's Guide to a Christian Bar Mitzvah*. 1st edition. Family Foundations Publishing.

✏️ Notes

PART 3

Influence

Attitudes are contagious;
are yours worth catching?
(A saying my dad often used and I still love.)
Original: Dennis Mannering

Wherever you go, you leave something of yourself behind – like invisible dust particles of influence.

Are your comings and goings strategic and graceful? What do your particles of dust look like and what would you like your loved ones' particles to contain?

In Psalm 23, the Psalmist states that God leads him to restful waters:

The LORD is my Shepherd [to feed, to guide and to shield me], I shall not want.
He lets me lie down in green pastures; He leads me beside the still and quiet
waters. He refreshes and restores my soul (life); He leads me in the paths of
righteousness for His name's sake.

— PSALM 23:1–3, AMP

The first mention of the word "leads" holds much significance. The Hebrew word is *nahal* (naw-hal), which means "to run with a sparkle".

When you enter a room, your presence is felt and leaves a certain amount of impact. Do you desire that your loved one's lingering presence bears a sparkle?

This final part of eternal preparation will unpack the four phases that will encourage your loved one to value time and opportunities, and to flourish in his uniqueness and spiritual gifts.

Part 3 encourages you, as the sojourner, and your loved one to progress from the Dependence part to a well-balanced functioning state of interdependence. It may progress off-road on the way in the effort to be independent – to "do life" without others' interference. But alas, such a state is unstable and will hopefully motivate him to reorientate and to find a new zeal for life on the road towards functional interdependency.

The aim is to set your eyes on knowing the eternal Father and leaving follow-worthy footprints, a legacy that celebrates the true calling of humanity.

Phase 9:
13–18 years

CONTEXT

Wherever I look
gestures are luring
voices are calling
and I am standing
wondering
where should I go.
My heart is my compass
safely linked with Yours
I know where I must go
I now know true north.

Your loved one has now crossed over into young adulthood and will be exploring how to do life from an angle of new responsibilities and new possibilities, with an unknown freedom to choose. It is both an exciting and daunting season to enter.

This is the moving-on phase from being dependant to gradually living interdependently with the environment, others and the community.

What does this journey require?

Replacing the Scaffolding

The scaffolding between the higher cognitions and the emotional weight of situations and experiences are gradually being removed. It occurs as connections develop and become more secure. This is especially so between the anterior prefrontal lobes and the limbic system, as well as between the heart and the limbic system.

Initially during this stage, the development of the limbic system, which regulates the emotional brain structure, enjoys priority. The adolescent's emotions may determine his choice of response versus reaction, which indicates that the higher brain functions of logic and rational thinking (i.e. higher cognitions) are not yet fully developed or do not participate strongly in the decision-making process. By default, therefore, choices are made via an emotional interpretation.

A study in *The Journal of Neuroscience, 2016*, shows that an increase in reward-and-sensation seeking behaviour is linked to a possible imbalance in the maturation of the prefrontal cortex.

According to the MRI data, various brain regions involved with emotions during this phase mature at a different pace to the cognitions, especially in the sub-cortical and cortical areas,[1] i.e. maturation of the affective (emotional) brain areas take place earlier than in the cognitive areas. This can lead to difficulty in goal-orientated decision-making. The young adult may find it challenging to have the required impulse control when choosing responses or reactions.

An increase in the limbic system's development during this phase may result in restricted maturation of the prefrontal areas of the brain; again, this can lead to stronger impulsive reward-seeking tendencies. You see this often in individuals where rebellion is activated — especially when it comes to boundaries and limitations set by adults and authoritative figures. This might act as a trigger and catalyse dopamine addiction, often fed by social media and a "likes" dependency.

In June, 2024, Max Chang and Irene Lee from the University College of London published neuroimaging studies on the impact of internet addiction on the adolescent's brain development in *PLOS Mental Health*[2], "In all of the reviewed studies, when teenagers with internet addiction engaged in activities governed by the brain's executive control network (e.g. behaviours requiring attention, planning, decision-making, and especially impulsivity), those brain regions showed a significant disruption in their ability to work together compared to those in individuals of the same age without internet addiction."[3]

In adults, the aPFC (anterior Prefrontal Cortex) plays a vital role in controlling emotional reactions. It does this by down-regulation of the amygdala's role in emotional responses. The amygdala determines the action of choice when in danger: fight, flight or freeze. Bear in mind that there is also strong communication between the amygdala and the physical heart.[4]

However, the aPFC and its connections with the limbic structure develop relatively late in adolescence and may only reach maturity in the mid-twenties. Until then, emotional management is done mostly by the sub-cortical structures, and these produce strong emotional reactions, with limited subduing.

When the adolescent matures slowly or with restrictions, he depends mostly on the nuclei in the thalamus and the amygdala to determine the "appropriate" emotional response.

Hopefully, he will eventually enjoy healthy top-down rather than just "down" processing.

The Role of Hormones

Phase 9 is also a season of major hormonal development.

As mentioned before, age plays a distinct role in the frontal lobes' level of participation during emotional conflicts. Hormonal influence also has a high determining factor during this phase and deserves a closer look.

High levels of testosterone have shown to impact the collaboration between the prefrontal lobes and the amygdala. It will limit the function of the scaffolding and can hijack the necessary process of replacing the scaffolding with more secure connections.

Sex steroids (hormones), such as testosterone and estradiol (oestrogen), play important roles during emotional conflict and how the frontal lobes and cerebellar areas will handle such conflict.

During this phase, it seems that there will be periods of developmental spurts that interfere with other developmental needs. Due to this, inner conflict, as well as a high demand for energy, will put additional pressure on the already bombarded young adult. Pressures and expectations stem from peers, academics, teachers, coaches, parents and/or friends.

According to the paediatrician, John Hopkins, "'teens' need between 9 and 9,5 hours sleep per night because of a second developmental stage of cognitive maturation". The sleep expert, Laura Sterni (MD), states that teens experience a natural shift in circadian rhythm. This results in difficulty falling asleep before 11 pm. (A circadian rhythm is a natural oscillation that has 24-hour repeats, and it rhythmically coordinates biological processes.)

*Circadian rhythms regulate many aspects of reproduction,
including timing of hormone release, ovulation, mating and parturition.*
— LAURA STERNI[5]

If the young adult is sleep deprived, it may lead to depression, a sense of not coping, and may challenge the required development and functionality of the brain, including impulse control and other functions linked to hormonal stress (for example, sexual drives and/or addictions).

As a sidenote: The term "teen" describes the years between 13 and 19 and was coined in the mid-1900s in America. *Adolescent* seems to be a more popular term to describe the developing person in this phase.

Orchestrating the Inner Order

The cerebellum (the small brain) has been largely understudied and underestimated. Up until recently, it has been viewed as the area involved in balance and muscle coordination.

However, Dr Jay Giedd's research has shown that the small brain is very sensitive to environmental impulses. Just as you can be physically clumsy, so can the various brain structures also be clumsy in how they work together. According to Dr Giedd, man can be "mentally clumsy". It is quite significant that the one area of the brain that develops most during this phase is the cerebellum, and maturation may continue until around 25 years of age. Note that all the previous phases have played a huge part in the effective development of the brain to support this coherent state of balanced processing.[6]

The cerebellum's role then seems to include guiding the different intellectual processes — as should often be the case in an adolescent's life — in order to help find the best way to respond. The goal, then, would be for all things to go smoothly by taking into consideration the various aspects involved in a situation. It aims to find balance in how the situation should be handled. The cerebellum has to support establishing and maintaining inner order and coherence within an extremely busy adolescent brain. It will support the integration of context into the whole decision-making process.

This is the profound role of the cerebellum: the small brain that plays an important part in reaching cognitive maturity. According to Dr Giedd, environmental stimuli are largely responsible for the development of the cerebellum, which is a huge motivator for intentional input into the lives of our loved ones.

As mentioned before, the physical often manifests the spiritual. The same applies to this physical inner order rapidly being formed during this phase. Inner order can also be referred to as congruency — a harmonious functionality between various aspects involved in a specific task or orientation. Emotional congruency involves an effective agreement among the

> When the various aspects involved in interpretation and decision-making operate harmoniously, effective choices can be made.

limbic system, the prefrontal lobes, the heart and the spiritual aspects of self, including a healthy respect for each aspect's role and responsibility. Higher congruency should always lead to more effective functionality, and therefore stronger positive impact.

The Greek word *sunergia* means "cooperation, or working together". Spiritual synergy can develop "where two or three are gathered together" (see Matthew 18:20) with Jesus as their collective focus. Godly order and cooperation flow from spiritual unity. This is the same for the Church (Body of Christ), as well as for the individual (physical body). When the various aspects involved in interpretation and decision-making operate harmoniously, effective choices can be made. Impact will flow effortlessly and peace will guard his mind and heart.

Trust Father God for restored physical and spiritual synergy during this phase and the ones that follow, starting with the adolescent and slowly permeating into his environment.

Adulthood Versus Maturity

Brain development does not have specific dates or ages for maturation. The brain, as with the rest of the person, is on an ongoing journey to full maturity. It may often take the broken or spoiled individual their entire lives to reach this. Reaching a certain age does not necessarily guarantee maturity.

Peter Jones from the epiCentre Group at Cambridge University states that human development is on a trajectory, an ongoing state of growing.[7]

However, the age of eighteen brings environmental opportunities that may challenge specific brain areas to reach some form of maturation. It is the time to launch into life after finishing school, and you are presented with multiple choices that will impact the rest of your life. At eighteen you are an adult, but not necessarily a mature one. Maturity is reached when you:

- know who you are in the light of who He is.
- enjoy healthy emotional and cognitive congruency, are socially interdependent and can celebrate your unique identity.
- live life with gratitude, wisdom, a sense of purpose, being eternity-orientated, living to know the one and only God, and happily serving in His kingdom (more about this in Phase 12).

Support for This Development

Remember the ideal parent's description, Approachable, Dependable and Available? Such a parent has conquered the fine art of really listening. To truly listen requires an attentive heart, attuned to the needs of the one being listened to.

The impact of listening attentively, and feeling listened to, strengthens relationships and a positive communication platform. This is a requirement for the adolescent's healthy development. According to ASCD's study in 2020, Mary Helen showed that an adolescent's brain strongly benefits from regular meaning-making narratives.[8] Discussions around stories and how they can unfold should form part of regular conversations at home, with a safe space for various opinions and interpretations.

The adolescent's sense of self (identity), emotional regulation and what life is all about will benefit from such conversations.

The most important connections between the aPFC and the limbic system becomes stronger, and the scaffolding from the previous phases' stimulation can slowly be removed, giving space for permanent connection, full-brain decision-making.

The Role of the Heart as Support for Healthy Top-Down Function

Heart-rhythm patterns and stability influence the afferent inputs to the thalamus. This has a direct impact on the activity of the thalamus and on choosing which sensory data will enjoy higher cognitions, and which will not.

This also plays a role in determining what will be consolidated and what the emotional content of the sensory data will be (consolidation is the formation of long-term memories).

A healthy, active thalamus will have an effective frontal cortical area and motor cortex. It supports attention, focus, awareness and motivation. Healthy motivation due to healthy priorities will always support a good quality of life, as well as effective emotional processing.

The heart further "listens" and "hears"; it picks up environmental stimuli and communicates the data to the brain for regulation and further processing. This is done through the electromagnetic field and the impact on the HRV mentioned previously.

When regular conversations with your adolescent include discussions of stories, day-to-day happenings, news or other social occurrences, his physical heart is involved and so influences top-down brain development.

Again, it is good to see how the physical often manifests the spiritual. The impact of the physical heart on how you interpret external data manifests how you listen, view, interpret and discern with your spiritual heart. Your spiritual heart should filter through the truth. This is one of the main prayer points (keys) for this phase: to have a purified heart filter through which environmental stimuli as well as spiritual input can be processed.

If such a filter is still clogged up with past hurt or unresolved anger due to past trauma, it must be attended to. Narratives help to create a non-confrontational space where new interpretations can be formed, and some unclogging of the heart filter may occur.

> Stories often include: Who am I? (the question of the heart)
> As well as: Who are others (in this world in which I live)?
> And: How does the world work?

When considering the possible outcomes of a story, long-term outcomes and results will support the connections between the logical thinking of the frontal lobes with the emotional areas of the limbic system.

How you choose to respond will require higher cognitive processing in order to provide deeper perceptions and reasonings. An increase of responses relative to reactions will occur. (Reactions are mainly driven by an impulse- or reward-seeking sensation.) The choice of response, therefore, becomes more controlled as a collaborated whole.

Parents can provide spaces where they can regularly discuss various topics in a safe, open and honest manner. The parent needs to understand and respect that your child, now a young adult, is a human in his own right, with his own opinions and unique view of life. He has the right to discover who he is in this world, and to secure his position with his spiritual fingerprint.

To have provided a safe space for the "Why's" will now bear fruit in healthy conversations. "Why?" helps to have a context-seeking approach to life – understanding that there can be different sides and interpretations to situations (see the milestone of justice in Phase 8).

"Context" is the theme for Phase 9. Context includes understanding that choices have consequences.

There is a difference between concrete stories and abstract stories:

- *Concrete*: Focusing on the facts happening in the moment
- *Abstract:* Considering bigger aspects that may have implications on the outcome or can add to what is happening

The abstract approach includes philosophising, discussions, considerations, and exploring different angles – all within the "present space" of an Available, Dependable and Approachable parent.

Some Dangers in This Phase

The role and impact of social media is enormous, and data shows that there is a direct correlation between social media and anxiety and depression.

Young people develop different personas: one on social media, one when with in-person friends, and one at home. They are confused as to who the "true me" is.

One struggling 16-year-old responded to the question of why selfies are posted on a daily basis, "I want to portray a very thin, very happy and very cute person. It doesn't really represent me, but I'll be making another post like this tomorrow."

This young lady, and millions of her "friends" worldwide, are trapped in a lifestyle of pretence. They are scared to death (literally for some) that the "likes" will get less . . .

Another says that when she peels away all the "false selves", she does not like herself much. About the one whom she knows is "the real me", she says, "It is better to dream and continue to deny, than to face the 'real' me."

Self-loathing is the monster of this phase. If not addressed and processed, it becomes the default approach to self and the inner version of self. It becomes your loved one's self-definition. Sadly, this seems to be the primary motivation for the "pandemic" of the age, suicide.

Suicide: 703 000 suicides per annum.
Youth suicides: From 2007–2021, the rise in suicides from ages 10–24 was 62%. Suicide is the second-leading cause of death in ages 10–14, and the third leading cause of death in ages 15–24-year-olds, after accidents and homicide.[9]

It is therefore clear why preparation for Phase 8 is so crucial. Securing a healthy sense of self-love and regard can honestly save a life. Among our youth, the real-world pandemic is anxiety and depression.

In their book, *Hold on to your kids*, the authors Dr Gordon Neufeld and Gabor Maté explain the desperate need for the adolescent to be safely attached to his parents instead of being peer orientated.

"The parent . . . is a nature-intended pole of orientation for the child, just as adults are the orienting influences in the lives of all animals that rear their young."
— GORDON NEUFELD AND GABOR MATÉ[10]

For parents to hear the cry of an adolescent, even though he may try hard to conceal or deny this, is for him to have a healthy, positive relationship with his parents: being respectfully loved by them, for them to trust him in his development to interdependency, and to show him that he matters to them by listening attentively and being interested in his friends and activities.

Dr John Duffy strongly advises parents to create a home where there are no-cell phone days. Make those days count in doing life together: making food, hiking, creating art, doing hobbies and just chatting.[11] As a parent, you can be selectively vulnerable in sharing some snippets of your own past or current battles. Have the discernment not to burden him, but to create a vulnerable space to be real, honest and open.

During these connect times, focus can be placed on emotional vocabulary, on how it seems to impact identity, on where love and care should come in, and on gratefulness and the role it plays in how you approach life.

When listening with your whole being (as with your heart), the physical heart communicates with the amygdala to lower cortisol levels. This will increase oxytocin, which will support healthy empathy and bonding.

Dr John Duffy wrote in his book, *Parenting the New Teen in the Age of Anxiety*, "The job of the parent is to help them make sense of and integrate all they take in. And to do that, we must know and truly understand their world so we can collaborate with them. Our kids are in an undue degree of psychic pain, and they need an open dialogue."

A Teenager's Letter to His Parents[12]

Dear Mum and Dad,

Please stick with me.

I can't think clearly right now because there is a rather substantial section of my prefrontal cortex missing. It's a fairly important chunk, something having to do with rational thought. You see, it won't be fully developed until I'm about 25. And from where I sit, 25 seems a long way off.

But here's what I want my parents to know . . .

My brain is not yet fully developed.

It doesn't matter that I'm smart; even a perfect score on my maths test doesn't insulate me from the normal developmental stages that we all go through. Judgement and intelligence are two completely distinct things.

And the same thing that makes my brain wonderfully flexible, creative and sponge-like also makes me impulsive. Not necessarily reckless or negligent, but more impulsive than I will be later in life.

Please stick with me.

So, when you look at me like I have ten heads after I've done something "stupid" or failed to do something "smart", you're not really helping.

Adults respond to situations with their prefrontal cortex (rationally), but I am more inclined to respond with my amygdala (emotionally). And when you ask, "What were you thinking?" the answer is "I wasn't, at least not in the way you are". You can blame me, or you can blame mother nature, but either way, it is what it is.

At this point in my life, I get that you love me, but my friends are my everything. Please understand that. Right now, I choose my friends, but don't be fooled, I am watching you. Carefully.

Please stick with me.

———

Here's what you can do for me:

1. Model adulting.
I see all the behaviours that you model and I hear all of the words that you say. I may not listen, but I do hear you. I seem impervious to your advice, like I'm wearing a bulletproof vest, but your actions and words are sinking in. I promise, if you keep showing me the way, I will follow even if I detour many, many times before we reach our destination.

2. Let me figure things out for myself.
If you allow me to experience the consequences of my own actions, I will learn from them. Please give me a little bit of leash and let me know that I can figure things out for myself. The more I do, the more confidence and resilience I will develop.

3. Tell me about you.
I want you to tell me all the stories of the crazy things you did as a teen, and what you learned from them. Then give me the space to do the same.

4. Help me with perspective.
Keep reminding me of the big picture. I will roll my eyes and make all kinds of grunt-like sounds. I will let you know in no uncertain terms that you can't possibly understand any of what I'm going through. But I'm listening. I really am. It's hard for me to see anything beyond the weeds that I am currently mired in. Help me scan out and focus on the long view. Remind me that this moment will pass.

5. Keep me safe.
Please remind me that drugs and driving don't mix. Keep telling me that you will bail me out of any dangerous situation, no anger, no lectures, no questions asked. But also let me know over and over and over that you are there to listen when I need you.

6. Be kind.

I will learn kindness from you and if you are relentless in your kindness to me, I will someday imitate that behaviour. Don't ever mock me, please, and don't be cruel. Humour me, as I think I know everything. You probably did as well at my age. Let it go.

7. Show interest in the things I enjoy.

Some days I will choose to share my interests with you, and it will make me feel good if you validate those interests by at least acting interested.

One day when the haze of adolescence lifts, you will find a confident, strong, competent, kind adult where a surly teenager once stood. In the meantime, buckle in for the ride.

And . . . please stick with me.

Love,
Your Teenager

How do You Pray Through This Phase?

Pray for healthy coherence to be restored between the various brain areas as they develop at different speeds – especially in the cognitive and emotional interpretations.

Pray for clear and secure identities that have been (are being) distorted by the overload of environmental stimuli. Pray for stabilisation of his self-definition – to align with who Father God created him to be. A redeemed orientation.

Pray for effective emotional management required during this phase to be a responsible young adult and to enjoy life with positive friendships.

Pray for the understanding that the picture of his life also has a larger story and therefore his choice of behaviour has a long-term impact. That there will always be context required to have a full picture. Pray for the effective functioning of the cerebellum in orchestrating a balanced whole-brain approach to interpretation. Pray for whole-brain functionality and the development of whole-soul interpretations and decision-making.

Pray that his heart cry to really be heard will be answered by his loved ones, but that he will become intensely aware that he IS heard by his eternal Father.

Pray that he will be convinced that he really matters to the God of the Universe, the Creator of heavens and earth (see Psalm 139).

Pray that the heart will carry healthy messages to the brain, as well as to the environment.

Pray that every aspect of his decision-making processes will work coherently with the influence of the intuitive heart, the "Who am I?" seat.

Bless your loved ones in a weekly rhythm (such as Friday evenings) with the Priestly Blessing in Numbers 6:24–26:

> *The Lord bless you and watch, guard, and keep you;*
> *The Lord make His face to shine upon and enlighten you and be gracious (kind, merciful, and giving favor) to you;*
> *The Lord lift up His [approving] countenance upon you and give you peace (tranquility of heart and life continually).*
>
> *NUMBERS 6:24–26, AMPC*

KEY SCRIPTURES	
Ephesians 1:2	1 Corinthians 12:24
Ephesians 4:16	Matthew 18:20
Psalm 139	Numbers 6:24–26

1. The National Centre of Biotechnology Information on Brain Cognition in a research article in October 2016.
2. https://journals.plos.org.
3. *Internet Addiction Disrupts Brain Networks*. neurosciencenews.com Accessed June 2024.
4. Van den Berg, G. 2023. *A Change of Heart*, Chapter 10. 1st edition. South Africa: Suiderkruis Boeke.
   Dahlitz, M. 2017.*The Psychotherapist's Essential Guide to the Brain*. Dahlitz Media.
5. Sterni, L. *Circadian Rhythms*. https://hopkinsmedicine.org
   Neuroendocrine Control of the Circadian Systems: Adolescent Chronotype https://www.ncbi.nlm.nih.gov/pmc/articles/PMC4762453/
6. Giedd, J. *Inside the Teenager's Brain*. www.researchgate.net/profile/Jay-Giedd-2/publication/12807832. Accessed January 2022.
   https://www.researchgate.net/profile/Jay-Giedd-2/publication/12807832
7. Jones, P. Wolfson College Cambridge; https://www.wolfson.cam.ac.uk. Accessed March 2019.
8. *Study of meaning making narratives: Building Meaning Builds Teen's Brains.* https://www.ascd.org. Accessed March 2020.
9. CDC (Centres for Disease Control and Prevention). https://kidshealth.org
10. Neufeld, G., Maté, G. 2019. *Hold on to Your Kids: Why Parents Need to Matter More Than Peers*. Vermilion.
11. Duffy, J. 2019. *Parenting the New Teen in the Age of Anxiety: A Complete Guide to Your Child's Stressed, Depressed, Expanded, Amazing Adolescence*. Coral Gables, USA: Mango Publishing Group. John Duffy is a Psychologist specialising in working with adolescents.
12. © Wingens, H. 2020. https://grownandflown.com/letter-from-teen-to-parents/

Notes

Phase 10:
18–35 years

MOTIVATION

Life in all its vibrant colours of experience supports maturation. During this phase, your loved one launches into "the real world" with its multiple opportunities and its potentially intimidating challenges. How will your loved one "do life"?

The tools of the previous phases have equipped him to cautiously investigate the opportunities with an open mind and an eager spirit. He should know by now that he is not only encouraged to explore, but also to walk in wisdom and dependency, guided by the Holy Spirit Himself. Knowing who he is as a loved, valued and unique individual, interdependent in society, will safely launch him into this phase.

This developmental phase will challenge your loved one to move into and become more settled in interdependent society. He should gradually grow into stable rhythms of give and take, adding value and receiving support. An understanding of who he is in relation to his physical and social environment will support a successful progress.

Progress depends on the individual and how he relates to the other role-players. Phase 10 requires participation of all the parties involved in engaging a new member and aiding integration into a healthy, functional interdependent society.

With the role-players positioned, the newcomer should be aware of the risk of being either strategically engaged or feeling excluded from society and the opportunities offered.

To manage risk-taking well during this phase, a healthy trust base – with a solid grasp on his self-definition and regard for himself and others – will be required. This calls for the participation of the whole human, the body with its brain and physical heart, as well as the spirit with its mind and spiritual heart.

The Maturing Brain and Heart

By now, the scaffolding between the aPFC and the limbic system should have made sufficient room for secure networks between the various brain regions. This will continue into the mid-twenties.

Being aware that the brain is still developing necessitates further strategic prayer. As discussed in Phase 9, the cerebellum plays a huge role in developing a synchronised brain, and it will also continue to develop into the mid-twenties.

The stronger the connections and maturity of the various brain regions, the more developed decision-making processes will be. Whole-brain choices should include the input of the heart. The heart, the most intuitive organ in the body, feeds the brain, especially the limbic system, with relevant data that should be considered when making serious decisions.

The heart integrates environmental input via the electromagnetic field of about 0,914 metres in perimeter, and communicates with the brain and rest of the body via four different ways:[1]

- *Biophysical:* pulse waves
- *Neurological:* nervous system
- *Biochemical:* neurotransmitters and hormones
- *Energetic:* electromagnetic fields

The heart plays a vital role in decision-making processes. It is therefore worthwhile to consider your loved one's heart state regarding his self-definition (the question of the heart), his convictions ("truth") and his emotional congruency during this phase. Your heart carries your story – how you perceive life and interpret sensory data. Remember, your loved one's story is based on his interpretation of his experiences. This may differ to various degrees from what the truth is. That is why strategic and intentional prayers are needed.

Intuitive, heart-motivated choices should ideally be based on the convictions of a whole, not broken, heart. Motivations and behavioural choices are the fruit of deep-set convictions. They manifest in the following areas:

1. Social behavioural choices
2. Role and impact of environmental responsibility
3. Career choices
4. Choosing a life partner and entering this godly covenant
5. How and what value to add
6. Study, after school education, work
7. Lifestyle, especially the three 'Fs': **F**aith, **F**inances, **F**riends.

Faith: Faith is the main source and provides guidance, purpose, wisdom and truth. Faith is not simply a mindset; it is a relationship with the one and only God of the Universe in His triune state of Father, Son and Holy Spirit. What and in whom your loved one believes will determine the direction in which his life goes, including eternity.

Finances: How your loved one manages finances (whether rich or poor) will determine almost every area of his influence sphere and plays a determining role in how he manages others and life, including his faith. Is he bitter, does he feel "done in" and that "everyone owes me"? Or is he rich and feels superior, stingy or cheats and plays financial games not acceptable to God? If you find that he battles either way in this area, pray earnestly that his relationship with money and riches will be transformed into being God-honouring.

Friends: The previous 'Fs' will again play a determining role in who he chooses as friends, the quality of his friendships, and how he regards other's time and input. You understand how destructive friendships can hijack your loved one's life. Therefore, pray that he will attract solid and safe friends and avoid those who have ulterior motives – like wolves in sheep's clothing. This will include the broken; often your loved one will have to discern supporting and comforting versus being manipulated and caught in the snare of co-dependency.

To be teachable, humble and full of appreciation towards God, his blessings and friends should be a non-negotiable characteristic in your loved one's life.

The Joy and Responsibility of Social Integration

During this phase, the calling from Phase 8 manifests and interdependency escalates, having the potential to bring great joy and fulfilment to the individual.

Some well-known Bible characters entered their spiritual careers while in this phase:

- King David was 30 years old when he became king (see 2 Samuel 5:4).
- Joseph was 30 years old when he became Pharaoh's Prime Minister (see Genesis 41:46).
- Paul (then Saul) was 30 to 33 years old when he started his ministry with the stoning of Stephen – although still misguided (see Acts 7:54-60).
- The Lord Jesus was about 30 years old when He started His Ministry and triumphantly completed His redemptive work at the age of 33 (see Luke 3:23).
- Rabbis start their ministry at 30 years of age.

It is also interesting to note that all the disciples were in this phase (or even younger) when Jesus called them. This is quite significant, as it runs parallel to brain development during this phase.

How great was the impact of their choices to leave everything behind and follow their Master? What motivated them to choose Him instead of following their own worldly dreams and goals?

And He said to them, "Follow Me [as My disciples, accepting Me as your Master and Teacher and walking the same path of life that I walk], and I will make you fishers of men." Immediately they left their nets and followed Him [becoming His disciples, believing and trusting in Him and following His example].

— MATTHEW 4:19–20, AMP

"Follow" (the Greek word is *akolouthéō*) is used as a particle of union, to accompany or be in the same way with who or whatever is being followed.

Your focus, the one whom you follow, is potentially demanding, but there's a willingness that provides energy. This unity will bring harmony, peace and an escalation in effectiveness.

The energy behind making big or small decisions is the momentum that activates choice – flowing into behaviour (inner), and flowing into impact (outer). Behaviour makes your inner world visible.

When the individual understands context (Phase 9), as well as how choices have consequences, he will have an enormous advantage in decision-making.

Research stretching over ten years (2016) has shown that in general, those in their 20s have more *quantity* friendships, whereas in their 30s, *quality* friendships carry more value and enjoy more intentional time and focus.[2]

The social experiences during Phase 9 will set the tone for the type of friendships developed during this phase. This is the phase where long-term choices are made:

1. *Life partner:* who you choose and the moral life choices of marriage versus living together/partners, for example.
2. *Career choice:* pre-career choice planning; studying and preparation.
3. *Where to settle/live:* planning of the next five to ten years or more, accepting seasons of change and adapting to change.

The "Why?" plays a huge role in the decision-making process. It exposes deep-set motivation and also primary priorities. Again, this flows from your "truth", as perceived in your heart, i.e. your convictions.

The "Why's" are formed by perceptions, which were formed during the previous phases of development. Perceptions are formed by inherited data (genetic information), experiences and values developed through upbringing.

"Motivation" is therefore the theme of this phase. Motivation is the "Why?" energy behind every decision, including primary (foundational) decisions:

1. What do I expect in life?
2. Why am I here on this planet. What is my purpose?
3. What standard of living would I like to have?
4. How do I view life?
5. How do I view others?
6. How do I view myself? What is my self-definition at this stage in life? It will adapt as you journey further on your path of life with new experiences, exposures and challenges.
7. How do I view God and faith?

Priorities are the hierarchy of what matters to you.

Motivation is determined by priorities.
Priorities are determined by convictions.
Convictions are determined by experiential and inherited data.
New redeemed experiential data will realign convictions.
Realigned convictions will change priorities.
New priorities will determine motivation to action.

Let your behaviour manifest renewed and aligned inner motivation.

The Two Main Motivators

Motivation (the "Why?" energy) is exactly this – a catalyst for processes (of thoughts) to be put into action. Every area in your life during Phase 10 is activated by deeper motivation or inspiration.

There are basically two main motivators: LOVE and FEAR – both are loaded with "Why?" energy.

When the main motivation is to *avoid* negative outcomes, the individual will make fear-driven or fear-motivated choices. Fear will also dictate the choices he makes if he wants to avoid the loss of something valuable or precious such as security, acceptance, inclusion, his goals, aims, dreams or success.

Love is *towards* something good and safe . . . not away from something bad and negative.

During this phase, where so many major future markers are chosen, it is vital to know (really know) his heart's focus and desires.

Is your loved one's heart focused on what needs to be avoided or is his heart focused on what is good, uplifting and praiseworthy?

For the rest, brethren, whatever is true, whatever is worthy of reverence and is honorable and seemly, whatever is just, whatever is pure, whatever is lovely and lovable, whatever is kind and winsome and gracious, if there is any virtue and excellence, if there is anything worthy of praise, think on and weigh and take account of these things [fix your minds on them].

– PHILIPPIANS 4:8, AMPC

The ratio for love versus fear should be at least 5:1. To strengthen a love-motivated focus, you must:

- Know who I am (the heart's question)
- Know my potential and strong points

Again, the physical heart manifests the state of the spiritual heart. Research in the field of Neurocardiology has shown how a state of patience, love and appreciation can alter HRV by strengthening it. The opposite states of anger, hatred and irritation can again lower HRV. A high HRV indicates a healthy emotional congruency, a sound immune system and a clear, focused ability.

Your state of focus indicates the attitude of your heart, which directly impacts your body, as well as the atmosphere around you. What a profound discovery of how the heart impacts and influences. Your loved one's heart matters!

This is also the primary determinant of how choices are made.

Context

The context principle, which we discussed in Phase 9, will further strengthen and guide as a main role-player in decision-making during this phase filled with new beginnings.

Context brings the now (the present time), the past and the future together.

Nothing is nothing. Never underestimate single moments. Everything adds to your context, interpretation and choices, like little dots forming a line. These support an abstract manner (instead of a concrete one) of viewing circumstances. A quick smile, eye contact when you greet someone – the big and the small choices are like pebbles in the water: actions impact.

Context provides an experiential reality to your choices and proves that action, reaction, sowing and reaping are unavoidable. It is the polarity you are exposed to every day. During this phase, your choices have a long-term impact. The ideal is to live a life according to the understanding of His Truth and His love, as it continuously unfolds.

Visualising this with your heart's eyes will support a lifestyle where the supernatural – God's story about you – becomes part of *your* story. Pray that God's story becomes your loved one's story too!

Your story is your heart's source and your frame of reference, providing advice and guiding your choices.

🔑 The Decision-making Process

Remember your birthright? Your right to be born, to live and to know the truth also includes your right to choose.

Part of the energy in life is this right. It is surely your biggest power, and it is also your biggest responsibility.

The mere awareness that one can have some sense of control over a matter or your environment, supports a healthy life-joy energy and motivation (the theme of this phase).

If we compare a person to a "company", most of the main decisions are made during boardroom meetings with the board of directors. The same brain areas are active even when the thought of a possible decision occurs before an actual decision is made and acted upon.

A person feels empowered with the thought that you can make a difference, however small, and have impact. This awareness is important when moving deeper into the inter-dependent section of life. For this to unfold smoothly, the various role-players in the psyche of man (the directors and their teams) need to be wisely managed and lead. "They" are the main motivators, guided by the "Why's".

Around the boardroom table, the directors will always include the Body, the Will, the Mind, the Emotions, the Spirit, and the Heart as the CEO.

However, if you look closely, there are other directors around the boardroom table as well. Every person's boardroom table will be unique in this regard; some might have religion, some self-pity and bitterness, some hatred, or anger, resentment or fear . . .

The important aspect here is that the heart needs to know its level of hierarchy and responsibility. So should the rest in order to function effectively. Dysfunction occurs when this godly hierarchy is distorted. Chaos will prevail without inner harmony, coherence and peace. Clouded judgement follows, leading to harmful decisions and limited impact, even removing positive influence altogether.

Disorder in the psyche's "company" will lead to wrong choices, wrong turnoffs on the path of life and wasting precious time and energy.

Without context, correct (healthy) alignment and inner harmony, a person will easily criticise opportunities, situations, events, others and himself. It will be based on assumptions that lack the "full" story (the context).

However, you serve a God who is a Re-Creator! He blesses your loved one with unmerited favour to return to harmony and effective coherence. His desire is for your loved one to flourish and to bless the community, to have fulfilment in what he does and how he lives.

Synaptic Pruning

In your twenties and into the thirties, the brain's development continues. The prefrontal lobes, as well as the connections with the rest of the brain and the body continue to be strengthened. As you know by now, the brain does not stop growing. Neuroplasticity is one of today's joyful finds: the confirmation that you do not lose the ability to grow new neurones and connections in amount and structure.

During this phase, there is an increase in white matter. White matter is the part of the brain consisting of axons, the extended connections joining the various parts of the brain. The grey matter (on the "outer side" of the brain) consists of the neural cell bodies and dendrites, the short connections. The grey matter includes the synapse areas and axon terminals.

White matter increases far more than grey matter during this phase. There is also an increase in myelin, which enables more information to be processed faster. The role of myelin is crucial in networking and interpretation. It insulates the axons and provides protection that enables faster, more efficient networking. Limited myelin has been associated with various illnesses, including MS and memory-impairing illnesses.

During this time of studying for and entering a career, the increase in myelin plays a vital role. As stated in the beginning, this is also the case in making crucial decisions that will determine the rest of your loved one's life.

It is incredible how Father God always correlates and recreates on a physical level, as He does on a spiritual level. The brain goes through a pruning stage during this phase; those pathways (connections) that have not been in use for a while are gently pruned for more available energy. A release of energy and capacity is thus provided for the more regularly utilised connections. This pruning is at the synapses of the neurones.

A decluttering, or cleansing, of unnecessary connections takes place. This is good and necessary but might "awaken" repressed memories.

When a person goes through trauma (type A or B), they may use "gating" to cope, especially when they are young. This is normal and helps the person to survive. Gating involves splitting the event from the emotion that the experience may have caused. An attempt to "deal" with the memory may have ended in frustration because some events might have surfaced but lack any emotional connection. Often clients will report watching a movie and experiencing intense anxiety, sadness or anger but lack any recall that might shed some understanding. Or they may elaborate on an extremely traumatic experience without the appropriate emotional response. Gating helps you to survive and carry on with the things in life as if all is "normal". It may include disassociation, using this creative but intense way of dealing with unthinkable abuse.

Healing takes place when both the valid emotions as well as the facts of the

> It is incredible how Father God always correlates and recreates on a physical level, as He does on a spiritual level.

abusive incident surface and can be handled together.

The ideal is to eventually revisit, confront and process the content of the trauma, to metabolise it and make a reconsolidated, healthy interpretation of the event. If this is not done, the information stays hidden and is not visited. It may cause a lacking or an irregular firing of neurones in those areas, which will then be pruned.

It is then no surprise that I often see clients who state that they have always coped with life until "suddenly" they are battling with various symptoms they cannot explain – nightmares, headaches, depression, anxiety, panic attacks, outbursts or unsubstantiated fears. I almost always correctly guess that they are close to 35.

How incredible our Creator and Re-Creator is to always be ready and willing to support this pruning. Jesus said to His disciples (also in this phase of development) in John 15:4, "Abide in Me" – as a branch abides in the Vine. This includes our complete dependency on Him for nurturing and support, to bear fruit that brings purpose, fulfilment, joy to self and others, and honour to your King and Father – your Vine and your Vinedresser (Husbandman).

"I am the true Vine, and My Father is the vinedresser. Every branch in Me that does not bear fruit, He takes away; and every branch that continues to bear fruit, He [repeatedly] prunes, so that it will bear more fruit [even richer and finer fruit]. You are already clean because of the word which I have given you [the teachings which I have discussed with you]. Remain in Me, and I [will remain] in you. Just as no branch can bear fruit by itself without remaining in the vine, neither can you [bear fruit, producing evidence of your faith] unless you remain in Me.

– JOHN 15:1–4, AMP

God states that you are pruned by the Logos Word that Jesus speaks to you. The Greek word for "prune" is *kathairo* (kath ah ee ro), which means to cleanse of filth, impurity, to prune vines of *useless* shoots.

A branch will battle to bear fruit if it has too many useless shoots pulling demanding water and nutrients. The little demanding shoots continue to drain energy and growth.

It is my true conviction that the only connections (synaptic) that will be pruned will be those in opposition to His Word. Experiences that contradict His true story of who you are will be pruned away. Remaining will be those challenging your convictions based on past experiences, now exposed and eager for healing.

God takes away the unnecessary "issues" or demanding lies that have been taking energy and making an unhealthy demand of cortisol in order to stay hidden or repressed. It leaves the immune system lacking.

You and your loved one need to be pruned regularly from unnecessary mental and emotional clutter, just as you need to be pruned of unnecessary relationships, connections, WhatsApp groups, social media connections, groups expectations, church-related groups that categorise and pressurise you, and so on. You need to get cleaned up! Pray this pruning for your loved one too.

Physical *and* emotional and spiritual pruning is necessary. Pray that your loved one's heart will welcome this process and continue to surrender to His cleansing – especially by His Word – His truth and wisdom.

Prayer for Phase 10

My Father, You are holy, good and powerful. It is an incredible joy to love and serve You.

Thank you for breaking open the truth about pruning. I see the grace in this and understand how necessary regular pruning is to unclutter and clear out my heart and mind. I also understand that, especially during this phase, physical pruning might stir up repressed trauma. I welcome and pray for safe, healthy and godly pruning – leaving no damage (by retraumatising) and creating space for Your truth.

My King, let Your precious Holy Spirit help _____ to expose any suppressed trauma so that it will be effectively processed. (If your loved one has not yet reached this phase, pray for the effective metabolising of past trauma prior to this phase and that it will not cause any long-term harm.)

Father God, may Your beauty and truthful reflection replace the distorted image of self in _____'s heart.

I now bring the three Lifestyle 'Fs' of _____'s life before You:

May _____'s faith be secured in Your Truth and the full redemptive work of Jesus, _____'s Redeemer.

May _____'s choice of friends bring him great joy and fulfilment and that _____ will choose wisely and discern with a redeemed heart who to engage with and who to stay away from. That he will know when to open his "gate" to others and when to keep them safely outside.

May peace stand at _____'s heart gate.

May _____ view and handle finances with integrity, with sharpness and with the fear of the Lord as a foundation. May _____'s financial management be aligned with Your will and plan for _____'s life.

I also pray for favour and the blessings of Deuteronomy 28 over _____'s three Lifestyle Fs.

Father God, my heart belongs to You, and I now ask that _____'s inner boardroom space will be realigned. I ask Your Holy Spirit to assist _____ that all _____'s non-original directors of self will be fired and that the original board will continue to be part of the decision-making process, synchronised with Your truth.

I pray that Your precious Holy Spirit will be the main Counsellor for the board of directors in the Heart Company of _____.

Thank you that You integrate _____ into a healthy season of bonding, exploring life and enjoying the freedom that comes with this phase.

May _____ also choose to follow You, Lord Jesus, as Your Spirit calls – in the community, in friendship circles, in church, family and in work.

In Jesus' mighty Name, Amen.

KEY SCRIPTURES	
Ecclesiastes 3:11	Isaiah 61
Romans 8:28	John 15
2 Samuel 5:4	Genesis 41:46
Luke 3:23	Matthew 4:19–20
Philippians 4:8	

1. McCraty, R., Atkinson, M., Tomasino, D. 2003. *Modulation of DNA Conformation by Heart-focused Intention, HeartMath Research Center, Institute of HeartMath*, Publication No. 03008. Boulder Creek, CA. http://www.aipro.info/drive/File/224.pdf
2. *In Your 20s it's Quality, in Your 30s it's Quality: The Prognostic Value of Social Activity Across 30 years of Adulthood.* www.ncbi.nlm.nih.gov/articles/PMC4363071/. Accessed March 2016.

✏️ **Notes**

Phase 11:
35–55 years

INVESTMENT

Settled in, enjoying lifestyle rhythms with family and friends, gaining ground in impact and getting to know Him better!

This is what this phase should look like. What can be done if it doesn't, or if things have turned horribly sideways and life has shown a different cruel reality? Then pray, trust and see! For you, as the intercessor for your loved ones, this may be a phase that is still lying ahead; for others, you might find that restorative prayer is required. Hopefully you have already witnessed an incredibly creative God at work in the lives of your family. Position yourself again in your most honourable calling, interceding for your loved ones and for those whom the Father places on your heart.

 **Adulting**

This is the phase of mature adulthood. Physical, emotional and mental maturity should be reached by now, especially around the age of 45. Spiritual maturity will continue as the person settles into the Truth and continues to abide in Him and gets to know Him.

Frederick Douglass, an American social reformer, born in 1818 in Maryland, USA, said, "It is easier to build strong children than to repair broken men." He also said, "The soul that is within me, no man can degrade." A profound statement.

Broken men versus strong mature influencers will manifest during this phase.

To be mature includes understanding how to love wisely – sacrificing self as well as celebrating the gifts with which Father God created you. It is often a challenge to balance these two poles. This parenting phase includes building a new generation (40 years), a new generation from being dependent, through efforts of independency into full interdependency. Life has now come full circle, from being parented to being a parent, and in the sense of training or discipling others in the community or at work.

Parenting includes caring for others who are still maturing, or the community's vulnerable ones, as well as the environment and general community. Caring is providing for others according to their reasonable needs and within the boundaries of your responsibility. This will include emotional, physical and spiritual care.

To correctly parent, you have to understand the concepts of caring, nurturing, teaching, loving and keeping the other accountable. Parenting will always include discipline. If discipline is done from a foundation of unconditional love, positive growth and transformation is likely to be the result. If discipline is done from a place of conditional "love" and "acceptance", it may result in rebellion and a resistance to change, "If you behave and listen to me, then you are a good (love-worthy) child . . ."

The psychological definition for a parenting role includes three major goals:

1. Ensuring children's health and safety in all three areas: physical, emotional and spiritual.
2. Preparing children for life as productive adults; to successfully reach this phase.
3. Transmitting cultural values, as long as the primary culture is as God intended.

A high-quality parent-child relationship is critical for healthy development (as discussed in previous phases).

The biblical meaning of parenting is explained in *Gentle Christian Parenting*[1]: "The role of the parent is to be a good steward of the children God has placed into their care." Three biblical truths are:

1. You do not own your children; God alone gave them the breath of life (see Ezekiel 18:4; Psalm 24:1).
2. Raising children is a deeply emotional experience (see Proverbs 10:1).
3. Parenting includes letting go (see Genesis 2:24).

> Ephesians 6:4, AMP: ". . . but bring them up [tenderly, with lovingkindness] in the discipline and instruction of the Lord".
>
> Proverbs 22:6; 2 Timothy 3:15, AMP: "Train up a child in the way he should go, and when he is old, he will not depart from it".

Parents have a responsibility to care for the spiritual, emotional and physical well-being of their children. Most importantly, the biblical duty of a parent is to teach their children about Jesus and His redemptive works in action and words. He needs to be a worthy role model, to be follow-worthy. Remember, your behaviour is a mirror revealing his worth, "Am I attention and respect-worthy?"

If parents or other role models do not follow through with what they teach, it can cause serious damage – not only in trust, but also in impact. Trust creates space and capacity for influence. If the behaviour contradicts teachings or expectations, it will leave the child (follower) confused and misguided. This could lead to anger, rebellion and a distorted sense of self.

A child will follow a parent when he feels respectfully loved and encouraged to be authentic in discovering life.[2]

I am the Good Shepherd. The Good Shepherd lays down His [own] life for the sheep.

– JOHN 10:11, AMP

Now may the God of peace [Who is the Author and the Giver of peace], Who brought again from among the dead our Lord Jesus, that great Shepherd of the sheep, by the blood [that sealed, ratified] the everlasting agreement (covenant, testament), strengthen (complete, perfect) and make you what you ought to be and equip you with everything good that you may carry out His will; [while He Himself] works in you and accomplishes that which is pleasing in His sight, through Jesus Christ (the Messiah); to Whom be the glory forever and ever (to the ages of the ages). Amen (so be it).

– HEBREWS 13:20–21, AMPC

(THIS WILL BE PART OF THE PRAYER FOR THIS PHASE AS WELL.)

Jesus is always the ultimate follow-worthy Saviour. A shepherd leads with respect and love, strength and wisdom, having a clear understanding of what is negotiable and what is non-negotiable.

I am daily and forever grateful for my follow-worthy God and Saviour!

To be a good parent and life-guide, as required during this phase, you need to be secure in who you are (the quest of the heart). A secure and healthy self-definition and regard will enable the new parent to care wisely.

To Love Wisely

The parental phase includes serving and loving wisely – not only the core circle of family, relatives and friends, but also the broader kingdom family, the community and even the outer circles of the environment. The parent is also a spiritual father/mother with spiritual children, requiring much wisdom. Be reminded of the theme of this whole prayer journey:

I have no greater joy than this, to hear that my [spiritual] children are living their lives in the Truth.

– 3 JOHN 1:4, AMP

When we truly love others without condition, without strings, we help them feel secure, safe, validated and affirmed in their essential worth, identity and integrity.

– STEPHAN COVEY

To love wisely is the key to flourishing in this phase. What does this mean?

1. It is the verbal and non-verbal "you-matter" language.
2. John 14:23, AMP: "If anyone [really] loves Me, he will keep My word (teaching)."
3. Matthew 22:37–39: Loving God must manifest in obedience. Love is a verb, falling into a rhythm of doing life, interdependently coming and going.
4. It is caring tenderly, fervently.

5. Romans 13:8: Owe no one anything, except to love one another, i.e. you owe man love.
6. It brings the fruit of unity, celebrating each other's uniqueness but operating in harmony with one goal and purpose.
7. 1 Corinthians 13:2–13 is the biblical definition of love.
8. Love will serve unselfishly but with healthy boundaries (see Galatians 5:22–23).
9. To love wisely is to be rooted deeply in love (see Ephesians 3:17).
10. To love wisely = spiritual maturity (see Ephesians 4:16; 5:2 – to walk in love).
11. 1 Timothy 1:5, AMP: But the goal of our instruction is love [which springs] from a pure heart and a good conscience and a sincere faith.
12. Loving wisely includes disciplining wisely and respectfully – never shaming.
13. To love wisely is fearless (not fear-driven) (see 1 John 4:18).
14. Serving the heart of others in a manner that makes them feel regarded, heard and safe in their uniqueness.
15. Philippians 1:9, AMPC: "And this I pray: that your love may abound yet more and more and extend to its fullest development in knowledge and all keen insight [that your love may display itself in greater depth of acquaintance and more comprehensive discernment]."

During this phase, the individual cares with an understanding of how to balance being selfless and yet to celebrate and regard oneself, to be considerate of others and to love effectively, to teach, guide, mentor and minister to the needy for the community, including school, church, neighbourhood and work partners.

Marriage will by default provide ample space to love wisely. Intimacy, the catalyst for multiplication, comes from the blood covenant between a man and his wife. From this unity flows powerful love and creative energy. Intimacy operates as a key that unlocks favour in multiple spheres of influence. Children look and learn the basics of relationships though their parents.

The godly unity in marriage should manifest in a strong intuitive perception for others. In Tommy Tenney's book, *Finding Favor with the King*, he highlights twelve protocols of the palace acting as Esther's secrets on how she won the King's favour and saved a country.[3] One of these protocols is, "Influence flows from intimacy, and access comes from relationship."

Wise love between a husband and wife will create space for influence. You set a standard through your presence, and the atmosphere around you will bring good and godly impartations.

To receive (enjoy impartation), attachments through safe relationships are required, which may require focused time, respectful listening and physical touch, verbal and non-verbal communication of regard and acknowledgement, as well as keen interest in what the other finds energising. This will bring forth mutual exchanges of love, and is the phase in which to invest and impart, pouring eagerly from your cups.

The theme for this phase is "Investment", with *love* as the primary currency.

The Vitals of Parenthood

A parent is the one who provides love, security and guidance, who influences with wisdom, yet is also the one who receives because of their investment. A parent understands how to love wisely.

Parenting should be love-motivated instead of being fear-motivated and avoidance-driven.

> **Remember:** An ideal parent is Available, Dependable and Approachable. Fear-driven parenting will limit the full potential development of the child, risking anger, rebellion, depression and anxiety in both parent and child.

A broken man is likely to attract a broken partner. These two broken people may have broken, fear-driven parenting styles, which could cause another dependent human in need of healing. And so the cycle continues.

The first four parenting styles briefly mentioned in Phase 7 were fear-driven, trying to avoid:

1. *Disappointment:* What if my child is battling in life, being emotionally, mentally or physically challenged? What if my child is not successful in academics/sport/music/socially (not popular)?
2. *Rejection:* What if my child does not like me as a parent, especially when I discipline or set boundaries? What if my child does not fit into his social environment, is not a leader or is not admired by others?
3. *Failure:* What if my child does not measure up to my expectations: in academics, choice of career, interests and lifestyle/partners, or to friends and friend's children's performances? What if my child views me as a parent who failed? Or what if I view myself as a failure as a parent?
4. *Danger*: What if my child gets hurt/stolen/abused/manipulated into harmful relationships or loses faith in God?
5. *Humiliation:* What if my child is ashamed of me due to my looks/weight/lifestyle/finances/social position/personality?

Every "What if?" carries a fear-driven message and needs to be confronted, prayed and worked through with the support of equipped others and the Holy Spirit. Fear must give way to love.

You serve a living Creator God who specialises in renewing and restoring, a God of transformation.[4]

The ideal parent (the fifth style mentioned in Phase 7) should enter parenthood with a heart unburdened from past pain and restored to godly alignment. He will then be a follow-worthy role model and establish safe bonds with his child. The concepts of God as a Father and a nurturing mother representing the Holy Spirit will create the ideal space for the healthy growth of his offspring. He will be available, dependable and approachable. He will know how to love wisely.

Alloparenting

In the broader view, it is important to allow the spiritual family to invest in our children's education and equip them for life. The community has a responsibility to parent the community's children.

Parenting should be done with sensitive discernment and healthy boundaries. This growing, interdependent phase should include a good example for the younger generation to observe and follow. The influence of the social environment – online and in-person – should not be underestimated. A broad community, in fact a global community, is involved in our children's lives today. Well-informed awareness is required to manage your loved one's exposure to it. The balance between exposure to global and societal inclusiveness and the present community involved is just as important for their development of wise interconnectedness.

If this is not implemented, the younger generation will continue to feel left out and will desperately seek to feel included. To belong is a basic need, first in the safe space of the core family, then moving out gradually into the outer circles of social exposure and involvement. Tasks in the household, socialising with parents, siblings and friends, as well as with other families when invited, are healthy ways of learning good socialising skills.

In a broken and distorted world, being a parent stretches far beyond blood relatives; it demands a strong community-involved adult.

The hierarchy in caring for the broader community should never overshadow the immediate family. To balance this is not always easy and requires godly discernment and sound godly boundaries. The motivation, the "Why?" behind the choices involved, should provide understanding and, if needed, rectify the choice of involvement.

Communal parenting provides a platform for collective (group) upbringing. It is very effective if the various relevant role-players offer their own areas of expertise. For example, if a father is absent, have various father figures who can support in the child's sport, academic or cultural activities. This is how community or church is supposed to operate.

In 2017, an article was written regarding the principles and need for collective parenting. A relevant question was asked, "Is this the future of humanity?"

A study was done in twenty-one countries, such as the USA, Russia, South Africa, Brazil, Grenada, Seychelles, and Chattanooga. The following statistics paint a very concerning picture[5]:

- 63% of suicides come from fatherless homes.
- 70% of juveniles in state-operated institutions come from fatherless homes.
- 80% of rapists are motivated by displaced anger, and come from fatherless homes.
- 85% of children with behavioural problems come from fatherless homes.

A global cry is heard from the hearts of our children. Will you turn your ears towards it?

Alloparenting can be described as a form of cooperative parenting within a community, to "father" and "mother" non-related young. Understanding that co-education is undeniably part of a strong community will bring collective parenting to a far more effective future-building position. Adults function as parents in various relevant areas of non-related children's lives. This strengthens the concept of community and forms bonds across families and culture. It is a powerful tool in every diverse environment.

Children are children, and caring parents are the same across the world. You are part of a global community, now more than ever.

Roy Bradbury said, "We are all cups, constantly and quietly being filled. The trick is knowing how to tip ourselves over and let the beautiful stuff out."

The Lord is my Shepherd [to feed, guide, and shield me] (parenting me), I shall not lack . . . You prepare a table before me in the presence of my enemies. You anoint my head with oil; my [brimming] cup runs over.

— PSALM 23:1, 5, AMPC, AUTHOR'S EMPHASIS

Father God – not your friend, your spouse, your child, your church or your work, money or home – is the Source of everything you need. Spending time with Him, restoring the connections and highways from your heart to His, is vital for the unblocking and free flowing of all your needs. From there, you will be able to provide for others.

Love-motivated parenting will not tire out; in fact, it will energise.
Fear-motivated parenting, on the other hand, may cause burnout.
Remember that fear-motivated parenting styles are avoidance-driven versus love-motivated, which gradually grows towards deep fulfilment, satisfaction and joy.

In June 2023, a study revealed that 57% of the 700 participating parents (with children still living at home) experienced parental burnout.[6]

A striving parent is fear-driven due to the expectations of the world in which we live, as well as our inner conditional acceptance. This spills out into our immediate environment – marriage, family, work. It is therefore logical that the children of burnt-out parents battle with mental issues such as anxiety and depression.

To be transformed from being a fear-driven parent striving for perfection (never to be reached) to a love-motivated parent requires some basic alignment – because an inpouring from a reliable source with sufficient available provision is non-negotiable. You are familiar with such a Source, but do you feel safely connected to Him?

And may the Lord make you to increase and excel and overflow in love for one another and for all people . . .

– 1 THESSALONIANS 3:12, AMPC

As you and your loved one desperately needed *inpouring* during the phases of Part 1 and 2, you are now in the phase of *pouring out* into a very thirsty community.

How Does Outpouring Work?

Have a look at the image of the mature mother/carer of her world. In her left hand she carries a container brimming over with fresh water to provide for her loved ones, and in her right hand, a lively sword to protect and to guide safely. She is a parent to many, a mentor and a guide. This woman is both carer and warrior.

Figure 11:1 Credit for drawing to *Kompas Gemeente*, Vanderbijlpark

How Does She Do This?

1. Knowing the right source

This alloparent should know the Source. She should be able to discern between the love source and the fear source – the two rivers from which we can draw and provide from for our loved ones.

The Love River should be the 1 + 1 = 2. This is the main source – no other source will suffice.

Spending time with the One, Jesus, as that Source of love is a non-negotiable for your role and responsibility as an interdependent mentor in this phase. Let His wisdom and truth fill your heart daily and provide all you need until it overflows.

> *Such hope never disappoints or deludes or shames us, for God's love has been poured out in our hearts through the Holy Spirit Who, has been given to us.*
> – ROMANS 5:5, AMPC (LOVE POURED INTO OUR HEARTS)

2. To be able to receive is another prerequisite for full functionality during this phase as an alloparent.

After the previous phase of synaptic pruning, the parent phase should be entered into with renewed space for this pouring in and pouring out.

If your inner space is still clogged up with unresolved issues of the past, limited capacity will cause an outpouring of "not-so-beautiful" stuff . . . and the ones receiving this will be left thirsty and desperate. This may cause them to seek other unsafe sources from which to drink – even if it provides only temporary and false love, acceptance, inclusion or belonging. When this happens, deception will be a familiar companion.

3. Enjoying the aligned position of being surrendered to Father God and His truth with your whole heart, your mind and all your might – loving Him and serving in His kingdom

This is a position of godly aligned authority and influence, understanding that complete surrender is the daily goal and the most sacred calling (see Psalm 23; John 5 and 15:10).

From this position, effective prayer and intercession will flow spontaneously. Part of being an alloparent is to protect and bless. This should only come with a deep understanding of what has just been discussed. There is an alignment with the Spirit's desires, and an anointing to carry it out. A partnership with Him enables you to lead well, to teach, to guide, to protect and to equip.

In Phase 10, motivation was discussed:

- Motivation determines priorities.
- Priorities manifest values.
- Values reveal heart convictions.
- Heart convictions are the fruit of your identity.

As your self-definition, your Who-am-I question (your heart's question):

- Aligns with your true spiritual identity
- His opinion of you and who He created you to be
- You will be able to enjoy the fullness of life and influence with eternal value

A parent – allo and biological – should never use their offspring or circle of influence to become their identity. Rick Joyner stated that children are not a parent's property, identity or fulfilment. These aspects should only flow from their unity with Him.

As you abide in Him, spending quality time at the Love River, in His presence, His sap will provide all you need as the branch needs to bear fruit that is God-honouring. This is the position of a surrendered heart. This is the position of a true leader.

4. Time management will also be necessary during this phase – knowing and discerning where to place focus and which things during the day and week are attention-worthy. Unhealthy boundaries and compromising values or godly priorities can easily diminish your inner resources. Time reveals your priorities.

Letting Go

Respect for the individuality of those you are parenting will encourage their natural move from dependency to interdependency.

Letting go includes the understanding of where this unique being's rightful boundaries are. Any effort from a parent type to continue parenting in previous developmental manners will confuse, project guilt and enable a false sense of responsibility in the child role when he has reached eighteen years of age. None of these will be beneficial to either role-player.

Letting go includes a willing encouragement to flourish in the next season. A mature parent will celebrate the milestones of moving into adulthood and eventually leaving his own follow-worthy footprints (see Phase 12).

The cycle is ongoing. Make sure that your loved one is in an energising cycle, joyfully participating in the healthy progression of his own offspring to beautifully mature and influence them. It is this parental phase's responsibility to keep the energising cycle alive.

Be careful that the cycle of life is not broken.

Prayer for Phase 11

Adonai, You are God Almighty. I can rest assured in knowing You are all-powerful.

You have created us to be spontaneous influencers. I want my loved one, _____, to make a powerful impact in the lives You have entrusted to him in this phase.

I ask You, therefore, my Father God, to increase his sense of discernment as _____ grows in wisdom during this phase. You are Wisdom, Lord Jesus. Please come and impart Your wisdom to him. Hear my pleas on his behalf to teach _____ wisdom and how to apply wisdom in this interdependent season of _____'s life.

May _____ be thirsty for You and only find satisfaction from the true Source of wisdom.

Father, I pray that _____ will still be strengthened in his godly identity, knowing and respecting his own, but also that of others' boundaries and the daily aligning with Your Truth. May _____'s priorities slot into the most effective rank, steering _____'s motivations, energy allocated and choices made.

My King and Lord, I bring _____ before You during this phase and ask that _____ will be sensitive towards his parenting role in the community, not only to be a parent of his own children, but to care for and guide those in his circle of influence. That _____ will be an alloparent in Your hands and under Your guidance. Through Your Holy Spirit.

You, my God, are the only living God, and I can pray with boldness because of the work of my Lord and Saviour Jesus. May _____ know true surrender and living in a very lonely and needy world. May _____ experience an ever-increasing dependency on Jesus as the True Vine, providing everything _____ may need to be God-honouring in this phase.

May _____ bear fruit that is fulfilling and God-honouring and that others will be drawn to Him by tasting _____'s life fruit.

Father God, may _____ experience daily alignment with Your Truth and his calling in the Kingdom. I ask You that _____ will celebrate the position of being a provider from the source of love and protect it with the Sword of Spirit, applying the Word of God in the right manner.

God of the Universe, may _____ be a godly leader, who guides, encourages, teaches, equips, blesses and protects; a leader who leads with wisdom and who loves wisely.

I ask You, Father, that the seeds of prayer and teaching will multiply greatly for the generations after _____, bringing great honour to You.

I now also bless _____ with the following Word of Hebrews 13:20:

Now may the God of peace, who brought again from among the dead our Lord Jesus, that great Shepherd of the sheep, by the blood the everlasting agreement. Strengthen (complete, perfect) and make you, _____ what you ought to be and equip you with everything good that you, _____ may carry out His will: [while He Himself] works in you and accomplishes that which is pleasing in His sight, through Jesus Christ (the Messiah); to Whom be the glory forever and ever (to the ages of the ages).

In Jesus' Name, Amen.

KEY SCRIPTURES		
Ephesians 6:4	Ephesians 4:13, 16	Psalm 127:3–5
Proverbs 22:6	1 Peter 4:10	Ezekiel 18:4
Psalm 24:1	Proverbs 10:11	Genesis 2:24
1 Timothy 1:5	1 John 4:18	Philippians 1:9–10
Psalm 23	John 5; 15:10	John 10:11
Hebrews 13:20–21	3 John 1:4	John 14:23
Matthews 22:37–39	Romans 13:8	Romans 5:5
1 Corinthians 13:2–13	Galatians 5:22–23	Ephesians 3:17
Ephesians 5:2	1 Thessalonians 3:12	

1. *Christian Parenting.* https://www.christianparenting.org
2. Neufeld, G., Maté, G. 2019. *Hold on to Your Kids: Why Parents Need to Matter More Than Peers.* Vermilion.
3. Tenney, T. 2003. *Finding Favor Preparing For Your Moment in His Presence with the King.* Bethany House Publishers.
4. Van den Berg, G. 2023. *A Change of Heart.* 1st edition. South Africa: Suiderkruis Boeke.
5. William, M., Kenkel, A., Perkeybille, C., Carter S. 2018. *The neurobiological causes and effects of Alloparenting.* https://www.ncbi.nlm.nih.gov/pmc/articles/PMC5768312/.
6. Chasing Perfection: Unrealistic Parental Goals Causes Burnout. neuroscience.com. May 8, 2024. University of Ohio.

✏️ **Notes**

Phase 12:
55 years plus –
End of the Earthly Journey

LEGACY

How powerful are the prayers of a man whose petitions have reached his children, grandchildren, great-grandchildren, great-great-grandchildren, and great-great-great-grandchildren. We are all beneficiaries of his devotion.
– DR JAMES DOBSON, YOUR LEGACY: THE GREATEST GIFT

I have no greater joy than this, to hear that my [spiritual] children are living their lives in the Truth.

– 3 JOHN 1:4, AMPC

Oh, how our hearts should cry out with this desire, for the culmination of all our preparations, a whole heart fully returning to the ultimate legacy! May your spiritual children live their lives in the Truth.

Let us change the known motto of "Life is too short" to "Eternity is too important".

This final phase is the ultimate time to influence with eternity in mind. What footprints do you or would your loved one desire to leave behind for others to follow?

Strategy in Prayer

Never underestimate your prayers during this phase. It is a future-orientated season, being mindful of preparing a legacy of eternal value.

The key question here is, "Where will your footprints lead others? Will they be follow-worthy, guiding the follower closer to the Father's heart?"

Footprints should provide clear directions to others. As they follow, your guidance should draw them even closer to Father God – drawing them in a godly direction without wasting time and energy with false hope.

A godly inheritance is provided through steadfast prayers and a follow-worthy lifestyle. Remember, the journey of legacy and impact stretches far beyond mere blood relatives (see the principles of alloparenting in Phase 11).

Layers of influence flow from your interceding prayers and extend into manifold future generations:

1st layer: Pray and desire that you, as the prayer warrior, will really KNOW Him – to perceive, recognise, understand Him and be constantly transformed to His Truth; to align accordingly; to remove the lies and replace it with Truth. This knowing should be the heart's deepest desire, intentionally pursuing His heart. In this phase, the heart's primary question and the core question on this journey, "Who am I?", should find its pinnacle point. You should KNOW who you truly are in knowing who He truly is, the pure and complete, ultimate I AM. The first aspect of Phase 12 is "Knowing Him" – knowing yourself. Knowing Him will enable knowing you, settled and safely rooted in His love. The answer of "Who-am-I?" lies in the great I AM THAT I AM (see Exodus 3:14).

2nd layer: Pray for the next generation, your children. As you embark on this prayer journey, your heart has already declared your willingness and hunger for more aligned and spiritually equipped children.

3rd layer: Pray for the broader generations – children of communities and other loved ones.

4th layer: Pray for the following generations – those born and those still to be born.

5th layer: Pray for the hurting generation – being global-minded.

This journey is therefore *Preventative* (in preparation) and *Redemptive*. These layers of prayer keep the prayer altars burning, bringing a sweet fragrance before the Father's throne.

To pray effectively should ideally be from a pure and whole heart and a sound mind, being able to hear the Spirit's promptings and guiding. Sometimes you will be praying in the nighttime or declaring Word over those He brings to your remembrance at odd times.

A prayer warrior is dependant, surrendered like the branch on the vine; he is willing to fully trust the Father. Because you can never be perfect, and often battle to juggle all the glass balls of life's demands, you almost always need His gentle encouragement that prayer is about Him and not about you. He is perfect and perfectly loving – enabling you to operate from this place of impact through His Spirit.

By spending time in His presence and beholding Him, you will see your reflection in His eyes; your true original self, redeemed by the blood of the Lamb, a victor (not a victim), able to create impact in the heavenly spheres. You are love-worthy because of who He is.

Intercession should be done with your understanding and then from your appointed position. By grace, you take your position and present your heart cries before your King.

Letting Go

Another aspect of this phase is letting go. Wisely selective release will unburden and free you for what Father has prepared to impart.

The second law of thermodynamics (study of action and temperature) states that all things move towards chaos – or a lower state of order. As things age, it takes more energy to uphold the order, or these things will simply fall into chaos. Entropy (the degree or measurement of disorder) always increases as we grow older. The body's available energy steadily decreases and needs more and more outside assistance to enjoy the "normal" levels of before.

This is true for your home, friendships, work and your walk with Father God. It all needs constant support. This "container" will require increased attention and deliberate strategies to maintain and enjoy a full and meaningful life during this phase. Part of a refocus is to utilise energy effectively and let go of some aspects.

This Letting-Go phase provides the opportunity to redefine roles and responsibilities, to be delivered of negative backlog and to embrace reorientation as a legacy-minded guide for others. Letting go includes:

1. Career-wise, the role and responsibilities will change significantly during this phase. It may be necessary for you to let go of certain daily and weekly rhythms that have been part of your life for years. If your identity has mainly

been built on such rhythms of work and family/socials/lifestyle, it will be a challenge to redefine "Who am I?" without my work, my title and position, my direct authority at work or home, etc.

This shift will be gradual but requires an intentional readjustment towards a more appropriate way of life, more aligned with the season you are in.

The Word provides no indication of retirement, but it does advise you to wisely adjust how you are going to spend your time and skills. Strategic adjustment will add great value to your life's quality and fulfilment in this phase. It will also shape your legacy.

Phase 12 presents a season of great potential in learning new skills, pursuing your passions and being available to support others, including loved ones and communities.

It is now clear that aging does not necessarily include lower or slower cognitive ability. In fact, more studies have shown how adjustable and accommodating the aging brain is. As from the beginning of human development, it does require stimulation and sufficient support. The vast amount of data stored in the brain of a person in this phase increasingly requires an ability to filter through and only recall the most appropriate.

"We now have neurological evidence showing that with age comes wisdom and that as the brain gets older, it learns to better allocate its resources," explained Dr. Oury Monchi, a Professor for Clinical Neuroscience during a clinical study at the University of Montreal (2011).

These studies further show that maturing brains process incoming data more sufficiently. It seems that the brain of an older individual will adjust in a less reactive manner and have more patience with others and circumstances. Maturity understands that making mistakes are part of doing life and not a negative mark against your name. The aging brain enables cognitive maturation. Again, our Creator God has prepared man physically to function in the theme of the phase, "wisdom".

> Positive feelings and having an enthusiastic approach to life play an enormous role in brain health.

To further support the neuroplasticity of the aging brain, Meredith Shafto and team provided data on how the aged brain becomes more flexible and synchronises with the various relevant brain regions. Such cognitive harmony is due to an increase of myelin and a now strong network that supports effective processing and interpretation. It seems that both hemispheres are well utilised during interpretation and decision-making during this phase.[1]

According to Professor Monchi's study with various age groups, those over 60 years of age appear to choose cognitive paths that save energy, without compromising context.[2] This may be due to an ability to eliminate the clutter and unnecessary information. Years of experience and a vast amount of already incorporated information supports this effective filtering, causing the person to make well-informed and thought-through decisions, as the wisdom of the aged.

Positive feelings and having an enthusiastic approach to life play an enormous role in brain health during this phase. Now is the time to cultivate healthy habits to enrich and accommodate our basic needs for friendships, intellectual stimulation and emotional congruency.

The *New England Journal of Medicine* has provided healthy tips to encourage healthy brain aging[3]:

- Don't be afraid of old age.
- Strive to develop intellectually.
- Learn new crafts, make music, learn to play musical instruments, paint pictures, dance!
- Take an interest in life, meet and communicate with friends, make plans for the future, travel as best you can.
- Don't forget to go to the shops, to cafes, to shows.
- Don't isolate yourself; it's a destructive practice for anyone.
- Be positive, and always live with the thought, "all good things are still ahead of me!"

And worth adding to this list: The greatest joy of this phase is to cultivate godly habits that will leave follow-worthy footprints for generations to come.

2. The hurts of the past; getting rid of resentment, bitterness and regrets.

So often this will include processing the disappointments and failures of the past. Life may not have turned out as you had hoped for, dreamed of and worked for. Marriage and relationship failures may have caused much pain, regret and loss. Broken or disrupted connections with children and grandchildren may have brought a deep pain of rejection and loss.

Sometimes this letting-go might require a grieving process – emotionally and spiritually metabolising the loss of that which will never be or never be again.

Forgiveness will form a vital part of this grieving process – it will release the individual to effectively let go. Gone is the bitterness, anger, and hurt, and all the choices and limiting fulfilment in response to this. Forgiveness will often include oneself – for missing opportunities, damaging or destroying relationships, or whatever else we might regret (see Ephesians 4:32; Colossians 3:13).

Asking the Father for forgiveness invites Him in to recreate something new – He always makes pearls from pain. Nothing is ever wasted when we choose to include Him in the details of our lives – the good and the regretful bad. When you choose to let go, to forgive, you increase your spiritual capacity for His Truth and allow His seasonal inpouring, which will most likely form part of your legacy.

Remember: Forgiveness opens the gates to the past for realignment and reconsolidation.

3. Redefining your role as a parent – this is a sensitive and challenging adjustment for most parents. It is, however, a very necessary one.

As you effectively move through Phase 8 as a young person and again as the parent of your own young adult child, this letting go will be more natural, although still painful and challenging. Just as those phases include processes of moving from positions of dependency to interdependency, it will also require adjusting positions in the larger family circle and society.

The dynamics of mother/father versus adult child and married adult child requires much discernment and wise love. As you might know, it is not easy, and therefore respectful and honest conversations will be very useful. A safe space to share hurts or disappointments will help this shift.

A parent of an adult child understands that his adjusted role will include:

- Being the praying parent for the generations
- Preparing to leave a godly legacy for the generations to come
- Knowing when and how to support the adult child, respecting the importance of him discovering his potential and ability to become a well-adjusted, responsible and value-adding citizen, fearing and serving God,

and being a kingdom-minded individual. To reach this, he will have to make his own mistakes, fail, succeed and grow at the pace that his capacity allows. The parent is no longer responsible for him — only to love him and pray for him — while still being an available, approachable and dependable person in his life

- Providing godly wisdom and advice, either when asked for it or when obeying a very clear command from His Spirit (such as a reprimand, a word of warning or prophetic word to encourage) — and only after a sufficient amount of prayer preparation
- Always communicating respectfully with your child as an adult and person in his own right, having his own dreams, callings, interests, tastes and opinions
- Enjoying and intentionally engaging or planning healthy conversations with your adult children. It should be a regular enjoyment and always viewed as a privilege and not a right
- Abstaining from discussing, exposing and shaming your adult children with friends, colleagues, Bible study groups or family
- Continuing to love your children wisely (see Phase 11), adjusting as time goes on and family dynamics change

Letting go means finding your full identity in being a child of the Most High. Neither your career, past or present achievements, children or their achievements, friends, financial success, lifestyle or spiritual position should be your identity.

As you spend time in fellowship with Him, finding your true identity is like coming home. This will spontaneously enable you to find rest. It is from such a position that serving the community should then flow. It will include a letting go of "self" and of all false identities, of who I am not, who others say I am, of self-resentment or rejection. Remind yourself often that 1 + 1 = 2.

Never use the love of God to justify your lifestyle. Use your lifestyle as a response to His love.

> Finding your true identity is like coming home.

Being grateful and full of appreciation will not only keep your heart's ears and eyes open, but it will also strengthen your physical heart and body as well.

To let go should be a gracious moving into the season of serving others with wisdom, kindness and well-managed time.

🔑 Multiplication

Now He who provides seed for the sower and bread for food will provide and multiply your seed for sowing [that is, your resources] and increase the harvest of your righteousness [which shows itself in active goodness, kindness, and love].

– 2 CORINTHIANS 9:10, AMP

Phase 12 is when the seed sown during the previous interdependent phases multiplies; there is an increase in influence through leadership, mentoring and equipping the younger generations and others willing to learn of your line of expertise. Impact will always include multiplication.

This is the phase of wise counsel – taking the lessons learned from past experiences and knowledge gained to produce a God-honouring legacy.

An attitude of gratitude and appreciation should be your heart's default state – creating a pleasant and welcoming atmosphere wherever you go. It will emanate from your heart as an electromagnetic field through your skin into the atmosphere around you.

When you carry this atmosphere, you draw others to you spontaneously and create effective space for influence – to mentor and teach. This is a phase where the limitations experienced previously are confronted, and you reach a place of living with renewed confidence to be authentic:

- To be the original person Father God created you to be requires knowing who you are (your heart's question) and being aware that you are constantly growing and changing – but keeping the core of your humanity
- To be able to discern scenarios and know where to add value and what value is required
- To enjoy the perfect balance between celebrating your uniqueness and serving selflessly
- To reflect His joy and love for others in such a way that they too will discover their originality in Him

Leave Your Sparkles Behind

The Lord is my Shepherd [to feed, guide, and shield me], I shall not lack. He makes me lie down in [fresh, tender] green pastures; He leads me beside the still and restful waters.

– PSALM 23:1–2, AMPC

We mentioned in the beginning of this final part that the word "lead" in Hebrew is *naw-hal*, meaning "to run with a sparkle"; to conduct, to protect, to sustain.

Sparkles shine and are visible even in the darkness. If you feel lost and confused, they will show you the way out.

Sparkles contain energy, they shimmer and glisten. Your physical heart confirms this by emanating your attitude into the atmosphere. An attitude of love, kindness, patience and gratitude impacts the space around you. Unfortunately, so do attitudes of irritation, hatred and bitterness. These are measurable in the electromagnetic field around you. Your approach to life impacts your world and leaves imprints on the hearts that follow.[4]

Dr James Dobson wrote in his book, *Your Legacy: The Greatest Gift*, "Give your children and loved ones a simple but profound message as you prepare to step into the next world, 'BE THERE!' If you accomplish that purpose, it will be your greatest legacy."[5]

The theme for this final phase is "Legacy". This phase brings the fruit of full development to others in order to provide sustenance and guidance for the hungry and the lost; fruit that realigns a godly position for inheritance, restores healthy bonding in relationships, restores discerning trust and respect, synchronises values with truth, loves wisely, lives with wisdom and leaves a godly legacy.

This fruit that brings honour to the Living God!

Culmination Phases Prayer

Our almighty King and Creator God, You deserve every declaration of honour, every level of admiration, every word of appreciation!

You deserve all the glory available; all power in every sphere and every heart cry of adoration!

It is an absolute honour for us to worship You, our LORD and our Saviour, Jesus! Thank you for completing our need for global and eternal redemption. We praise You with all our energy, our thoughts, our focus and our attitudes. We are completely undeserving, so it is an absolute privilege to place our single focus on YOU and soak Your beauty in!

Fill us today, Father God, with Your joy, Your love and Your peace. Increase our wisdom as we enter Your presence and bring this petition of our hearts before Your Throne of Grace.

Father God, from Phase 1, our desire is that our loved ones (biological and spiritual children) will live their lives in the Truth.

We therefore trust You to walk this journey with us in order to align with Your Truth in preparation for a new generation, and for the restoration and realignment of the history of our loved ones to Your Story.

We are convinced that You are not bound by time and can therefore move "back" in time to the harmful moments of our lives. You are able and willing to remove the distortions and confusions, the lies and the deceptions caused by trauma. You are also able to recreate the interpretation of those incidents so that the message it conveyed does not bring any more harm, but a redeemed version, Your truth regarding who we are, who You are and what life is all about – because You are the Re-Creator God!

Deuteronomy 30:6, AMPC, declares, "And the Lord your God will circumcise your hearts and the hearts of your descendants, to love the Lord your God with all your [mind and] heart and with all your being, that you may live."

Father, we pray today that we ourselves, our loved ones and those You lay on our hearts, will:

- *Receive and celebrate our birthright.*
- *Be secured in unconditional love bonds as the primary bond with self, others and with You.*
- *Be secured in knowing "Who I am" in relation to the world and not be intimidated or deceived.*

- *Enjoy healthy trust and discernment, which will enable us to receive life's necessities.*
- *Know we are welcome, safe and loved.*
- *Have JOY as our safe and default camp, securely established and welcoming to every return from an experience.*
- *Respect self, others and You, Your commands and precepts first and foremost and understand how respect is communicated.*
- *Be love-motivated, operating and making behavioural choices from the Love River (ratio 5:1 versus the Fear River).*
- *Receive the key of knowing self – the primary question of the heart – in the light of who You are.*
- *Have wisdom, including understanding, insight, the right application of knowledge, discernment and discretion.*
- *Have NO room for self-loathing, but will view and interpret experiences within context and Your light of Truth.*
- *Be motivated with love and awe of You, our YHVH God.*
- *Love wisely, according to Philippians 1:9–11.*
- *Know self by knowing You; gently letting go of past hurts and adjusting wisely to new roles and responsibilities – to be free to leave follow-worthy footprints for the generations to come.*
- *Lead the beneficiaries of our prayers and supplications to enjoy unhindered favour and fellowship with the King of kings, our Lord and Saviour through Your powerful Spirit.*
- *Strengthen highways from our and our loved ones' hearts to Yours!*

Blessed is the man whose strength is in the You, in whose heart are the highways to Zion (see Psalm 84:5).

Thank you that our lives are cherished in Your heart.

In Your Name, Lord Jesus, our Saviour and King, we pray! Amen.

KEY SCRIPTURES	
3 John 1:4	Ecclesiastes 3:11
2 Corinthians 9:10	Psalm 23:1–2
Deuteronomy 30:6	Philippians 1:9–11
Psalm 84:5	Ephesians 4:32
Colossians 3:13	Matthew 6:14–15

1. https://fitnessleague.co.za/the-brain-of-an-elderly-person. Accessed June 2022.
2. https://criugm.qc.ca/en/chercheurs/monchi-oury-en/
https://www.sciencedaily.com/releases/2011/08/110825102253.htm
3. https://criugm.qc.ca/en/chercheurs/monchi-oury-en/
https://www.sciencedaily.com/releases/2011/08/110825102253.htm
4. Van den Berg, G. 2023. Dr. *A Change of Heart*, Chapter 10. 1st edition. South Africa: Suiderkruis Boeke.
5. Dobson, J. 2015. *Your Legacy: The Greatest Gift*. NY: Faithwords.

Notes

Recommended Reading

Axline, V.M. 1986. *Dibs in Search of Self: The Renowned, Deeply Moving Story of an Emotionally Lost Child Who Found His Way Back*. Ballantine Books.

Axline, V.M. 1993. *Play Therapy: Vital Tool in the Growth and Development of Children*. Ballantine Books.

Banks, M. 2022. *The Secret Science of Baby*. Dallas, USA: BenBella Books. ISBN: 9781637741467

Chapman, G.D. 2015. *The 5 Love Languages*. Chicago, USA: Moody Press.

Cloud, H. Dr. 2023. *Trust: Knowing When to Give It, When to Withhold It, How to Earn It, and How to Fix It When It Gets Broken*. California, USA: Worthy Books

Covey, S.R. 1989, 2004. *7 Habits of highly effective people. Powerful Lessons in Personal Change*. Londen: Simon & Schuster.

Dahlitz, M. 2017. *The Psychotherapist's Essential Guide to the Brain*. Brisbane, Australia: Dahlitz Media.

Dobson, J. 2015. *Your Legacy: The Greatest Gift*. NY: Faithwords.

Duffy, J. 2019. *Parenting the New Teen in the Age of Anxiety: A Complete Guide to Your Child's Stressed, Depressed, Expanded, Amazing Adolescence*. Coral Gables, USA: Mango Publishing Group.

Gitt, W. 1999. *The Wonder of Man*. Bieleveld: Christeliche LiteraturVerbreitung. ISBN: 9783893973972

Goleman, D. 2006. *Social Intelligence: The New Science of Human Relationships*. London: Hutchinson.

Hill, C. 1998. *Bar Barakah: A Parent's Guide to a Christian Bar Mitzvah*. 1st edition. Family Foundations Publishing.

Kluger, J. 2012. *The Sibling Effect: What the Bonds Among Brothers and Sisters Reveal About Us*. Riverhead Books, U.S.

Levine, P.A. 1997. *Waking the Tiger: Healing Trauma*. California, USA: North Atlantic Books.

Morris, H.M. 2005. *The Genesis Record*, p. 86. Michigan: Baker Books.

Murphy, K. 2020. *You're not listening*. UK: Penguin Random House.

Neufeld, G., Maté, G. 2019. *Hold on to Your Kids: Why Parents Need to Matter More Than Peers*. Vermilion.

Tenney, T. 2003. *Finding Favor Preparing For Your Moment in His Presence with the King*. Bethany House Publishers.

Van den Berg, G. 2023. Dr. *A Change of Heart*, pp. 204–226. 1st edition. South Africa: Suiderkruis Boeke.

Van der Kolk, B. 2015. *The Body Keeps the Score: Mind, Brain and Body in the Transformation of Trauma*. USA: Penguin Random House.

Winston, R. 2004. 1st edition. *What Makes Me Me?* NY: DK Children.

About the Author

Gerdi van den Berg has been involved in pastoral counselling and cognitive behavioural therapy for more than 25 years. Her passion is to support people on their road to healing. She believes that people consist of body and spirit, with the spiritual heart as the core. These aspects of our being function interdependently. Unless you understand, acknowledge and repair the role that each part plays, you will not be able to function effectively as a person.

Gerdi obtained a BSc. degree in Biochemistry at Free State University, an Honours degree in Psychology at the University of Stellenbosch, and a Master's and Doctorate in Sociology (in the socio-cognitive field) at Trinity University in Delaware in the USA. During her studies, her research centred on socio-cognitive neuroscience, focusing on the social and motivational aspects of human behaviour, information processing and decision-making, as well as the various brain mechanisms involved in these processes.

Gerdi currently runs her own counselling practice where she offers pastoral counselling and cognitive behavioural therapy (CBT), both in-person and online. She also hosts several workshops and courses (online and in-person) every year.

Gerdi and her husband, Cobus, have been married for 35 years. They have three adult children and one grandchild.

Heart Matters Counselling and Training

For more research articles on the topics discussed in this book,
to find out more about counselling and training offered by *Heart Matters*
as well as Dr van den Berg's book, *A Change of Heart*, scan the
QR code provided above or visit www.heartmatters.co.za